NO TEARS FOR
BLACK JACK KETCHUM

NO TEARS FOR
BLACK JACK KETCHUM

Facsimile of Number 290 of the Original 1958 Edition

by
F. Stanley

New Foreword
by
Marc Simmons

SOUTHWEST HERITAGE SERIES

SANTA FE

Sunstone books may be purchased for educational, business, or sales
promotional use. For information please write:
Special Markets Department, Sunstone Press,
P.O. Box 2321, Santa Fe, New Mexico 87504-2321.

Library of Congress Cataloging-in-Publication Data

Stanley, F. (Francis), 1908-
 No tears for Black Jack Ketchum / with a new foreword by Marc Simmons ;
by F. Stanley.
    p. cm. -- (Southwest heritage series)
 Originally published: Rotan, Tex. : F. Stanley, c1958.
 "Facsimile of number 290 of the original 1958 edition."
 Includes bibliographical references.
 ISBN 978-0-86534-682-6 (softcover : alk. paper)
 1. Ketchum, Black Jack, 1863-1901. 2. Outlaws--Southwest, New--Biogra-
phy. 3. Southwest, New--History--1848- 4. Frontier and pioneer life--West
(U.S.) I. Title.
 F786.K44S73 2008
 979!02092--dc22
 [B]

                            2008022926

WWW.SUNSTONEPRESS.COM
SUNSTONE PRESS / POST OFFICE BOX 2321 / SANTA FE, NM 87504-2321 /USA
(505) 988-4418 / ORDERS ONLY (800) 243-5644 / FAX (505) 988-1025

The Southwest Heritage Series is dedicated to Jody Ellis and Marcia Muth Miller, the founders of Sunstone Press, whose original purpose and vision continues to inspire and motivate our publications.

CONTENTS

I

THE SOUTHWEST HERITAGE SERIES

The history of the United States is written in hundreds of regional histories and literary works. Those letters, essays, memoirs, biographies and even collections of fiction are often first-hand accounts by people who wanted to memorialize an event, a person or simply record for posterity the concerns and issues of the times. Many of these accounts have been lost, destroyed or overlooked. Some are in private or public collections but deemed to be in too fragile condition to permit handling by contemporary readers and researchers.

However, now with the application of twenty-first century technology, nineteenth and twentieth century material can be reprinted and made accessible to the general public. These early writings are the DNA of our history and culture and are essential to understanding the present in terms of the past.

The Southwest Heritage Series is a form of literary preservation. Heritage by definition implies legacy and these early works are our legacy from those who have gone before us. To properly present and preserve that legacy, no changes in style or contents have been made. The material reprinted stands on its own as it first appeared. The point of view is that of the author and the era in which he or she lived. We would not expect photographs of people from the past to be re-imaged with modern clothes, hair styles and backgrounds. We should not, therefore, expect their ideas and personal philosophies to reflect our modern concepts.

Remember, reading their words and sharing their thoughts is a passport back into understanding how the past was shaped and how it influenced today's world.

Our hope is that new access to these older books will provide readers with a challenging and exciting experience.

II

FOREWORD TO THIS EDITION

The Controversial F. Stanley
by
Marc Simmons

As a professional historian, I've often been asked my opinion of the author who wrote under the pen name, F. Stanley. According to his 1996 obituary, he published 190 books and booklets on New Mexico history, quite a record by any standard. The problem is, F. Stanley has been almost universally condemned for the innumerable flaws that litter his writings. However, behind the man and the work lurks a curious story.

He was born Louis Crocchiola in New York's Greenwich Village on October 31, 1908 to Italian immigrant parents. After receiving a Bachelor's degree in English at Catholic University in Washington, DC, Louis entered the priesthood in 1938. On that occasion, as was allowed, he formally added the new names Stanley and Francis to his birth name, Louis Crocchiola. Thereafter, he was called simply Father Stanley.

Shortly after his ordination, the young priest was diagnosed with the beginnings of tuberculosis. Following medical advice of the day, the Church sent Father Stanley to Hereford, Texas in the Panhandle, hoping the arid climate might cure him. It did! Something else occurred at the same time. Father Stanley fell under the spell of the Southwest, leading him to become one of the most prolific historical writers of his day.

In 1940 he applied for pastoral work in New Mexico, since he was fluent in Spanish and thought he could be most useful there. The Archbishop of Santa Fe accepted him, assigning Father Stanley first to the Guadalupe church in Taos and then to the San Miguel church at Socorro.

During the 1940s, he served six or so different parishes in northern or eastern New Mexico, thereby becoming familiar with rural and small town life. It was while stationed at Taos, though, that Father Stanley caught the writing bug through mingling with local authors. But later as he was transferred by the Archbishop from one parish to another, he would begin looking into the history of his temporary residence and compiling a file of notes.

His first book, *Raton Chronicle*, appeared in 1948. Then in rapid succession F. Stanley published full-length histories on Cimarron, Socorro, Las Vegas, and the Maxwell land grant. Soon to his line of books, F. Stanley added an on-going series dedicated to a single small town or fort that other writers had ignored. These little booklets remain easily recognizable with their canary yellow covers and crimson red lettering, plus the New Mexico state emblem, the Zia sun symbol. Eventually, these small works alone numbered 123 titles.

One of the earliest treatments of the historic and controversial Maxwell Land Grant was published by F. Stanley in 1952, titled *The Grant That Maxwell Bought*. Although other books on the subject have appeared since, serious readers still need to go back and examine what Father Stanley had to say. Otherwise, small nuggets buried in his pages, and nowhere else, may be missed.

Remarkably, F. Stanley personally financed all of his publications, often going deeply into debt. The several printers he used were generally tolerant of the delay in paying his bills.

Even more stressful for Father Stanley was the harsh criticism his writings received from historians and book reviewers. They unmercifully picked apart his unedited and untidy prose, pointed out frequent mistakes, and condemned the neglect of standards in the composition or format of his books.

For one example, a serious slip occurred in the naming of F. Stanley's longest work, a history of the New Mexico state capital in three volumes, titled *Ciudad Santa Fe*. Under the old Spanish system, Santa Fe in reality never achieved the rank of a *ciudad* (chartered city), but retained the status of a town (*villa*). The author had missed that pivotal fact and thus launched his three volume set with a conspicuous error on the covers.

In 1985 Mary Jo Walker, a librarian at Eastern New Mexico University, Portales, published a sympathetic biography, *The F. Stanley Story*. The book contains quotes from interviews given by Father Stanley in which he defends himself and his methods.

His main plea was: "Pardon the mistakes, but say a kind word for my effort." Painfully aware of his failings, he claimed that his intent was merely to assemble fugitive information from obscure courthouse records, old newspaper files, and archives so that others more able could pick up the thread where he left off and carry on.

After publication of Walker's biography, some historians, myself included, began to look more charitably toward Father Stanley Crocchiola. The fact is, despite his deficiencies, he managed to make in his own quirky way a not insignificant contribution to our regional history.

Today, F. Stanley books and booklets are worth collecting. I'm always happy when I can add another one of his to my personal library. I just wish he was still around so that I could tell him that.

Sunstone Press in choosing to include F. Stanley books in its honored Southwest Heritage Series is wisely making this book available again to the reading public.

III

A MAN'S REACH
"Take him for what he is worth"
from
The F. Stanley Story
by
Mary Jo Walker

It is difficult to say to what extent negative criticism and neglect may have personally affected Father Stanley. Some of his works in the 1970s showed considerable care in preparation, but no more so than his major efforts in earlier decades. He knew his own limitations as well as any of his critics did, but he believed quite sincerely that the flaws in his work were largely literary in nature and therefore of little overall significance; or alternatively that they represented realities over which he had little control, such as his limited time or the cost of typesetting footnotes. His first reactions may be surmised from comments in the foreword to *Dave Rudabaugh*.

> *I used to apologize for my mistakes. Come to think of it, why should I? I tried; that's more than my critics did. I investigated to the best of my ability, often going sleepless and hungry in order to attain the facts. No patron has come along the way. I had to rough it alone.... The book may not be literary, but it is factual. In the long run, truth survives.*

Two years later, in *The Duke City*, he confessed from a somewhat different perspective:

> *I am grateful for all criticism—constructive or otherwise.*

And in *Satanta and the Kiowas*, 1968, he pled:

> *Let my mistakes be my Calvary, and let my readers be*
> *my confessors from whom we hope to obtain pardon and*
> *forgiveness.*

Simply and with a kind of humble determination, he persevered for many years, his principal resources being his formidable drive and his eagerness to help preserve the history of the region he loved so well. No doubt he attempted too much; probably, as with so many of us, his reach exceeded his grasp. His hope, which he stated over and over again, was that his books would provide guidance for others and "prove a...contribution to Western Americana." That purpose and his dedication to it do not serve to be lightly dismissed.

Taken as a whole, with all its human flaws, F. Stanley's work stands as a unique contribution, as much a part of the written record "as Coronado's visit." Even Ramon Adams acknowledged that "he deserves a full measure of credit for supplying hitherto unpublished information," for putting something into print about obscure places and people, for adding to the body of recorded knowledge about the Southwest. Whatever the final evaluation may be, however, it is certain that F. Stanley has earned a place in southwestern history in his own right.

F. Stanley

IV

TRIBUTE TO F. STANLEY
by
Jack D. Rittenhouse
from
The F. Stanley Story
by
Mary Jo Walker
Albuquerque, New Mexico / March, 1984

Some historians write because they hope their writing will bring them money or promotion or tenure. Some write to espouse a cause. A few write because they must, because it is the only way they can quench an inner thirst or scratch an itch of curiosity. The last class is the happiest, and F. Stanley is in this group.

The term historian has many shadings. Among academic people, a historian is a certified scholar whose commission of rank is a degree of Doctor of Philosophy in history, and whose income results from full-time teaching or writing history. Some of these go on to glory and excellence in their work; some gain renown as researchers or as teachers, become a historian's historian, but find writing a difficult task. Many bank their inner fire when they don their doctoral robes and are content to plod along as routine teachers, living as comfortably as a toad in a puddle of buttermilk, looking upon their diploma as a union card.

The grass roots historian is another type, curious about people and places around them. Their writings are their only certification. Some become antiquarians, with a dilettante interest in ancient things and more curious about precision in minutiae than in the social significance of their subject. The term antiquarian has a different meaning among historians than among bookmen.

Still another type of historian is the buff, an individual who is an enthusiast or devotee of a specific subject. When it comes to sheer bulk of knowledge about a subject, or even to accuracy on a point of information, I have seen many buffs who outclassed Ph.D's. I personally know only three individuals who have their own microfilm readers at home, and all three are buffs. They travel great distances to look at a gravestone or a courthouse record, which is not to say that professional historians and grassroots historians also do not do this, of course.

We owe much to the grassroots historian and the buff. They are the prospectors who discover new lodes. They are curious about people and places and customs, combining the interests of the folklorist and the historian, and if they are good at what they do, they find their work accepted and even honored.

F. Stanley is one whose curiosity and inner fire has drawn him to the study of people and places and events that had gone unnoticed until he saw them. He advanced knowledge in many directions, lit many candles to dispel darkness.

His works are only beginnings, and he knows this. In a sense, history writes itself merely by occurring, and thus there is the axiom that history is not written but rewritten. Another New Mexico local historian, Fray Angélico Chávez, once spoke to El Corral de Santa Fe Westerners and said that history is not a static, pure thing that can be discovered once, written down, and preserved intact forever. Instead, he said, history is a living, growing body that must be nurtured...and which occasionally requires surgery.

F. Stanley has wandered across the Southwest like a Johnny Appleseed of history, planting seedlings in the form of booklets and leaving their later nurturing to others. Later historians will convert these seedlings into trees, by pruning, fertilizing and grafting. The work will require more research, more verification, correction and amplification. But F. Stanley planted the first seed.

The historian who uses only *one* source for his work is a fool, but the historian who refuses to review any source is an idiot. Any source may have errors caused by lack of information, or poor proofreading, or hasty writing. But some questionable bit of old-timer's lore may raise the possibility of truth; it is then up to the later historian to prove or disprove the fact. Once, when I was gathering information about the New Mexico ghost town of Cabezón, I read an old-timer's memoir that mentioned a stage line running through the town. Nowhere else did I find any mention of this, and I sought to verify the story. A usually reliable professional historian scoffed at the notion that the town had ever been on a commercial stage line. Then a museum curator found a printed timetable of the Star Stage Line, listing the route and showing Cabezón as a stop. Although many dissertations do not list F. Stanley works as sources, the padre's booklets have nonetheless been studied for similar possible clues. Given the time and resources, F. Stanley himself would have gone farther; he leaves that to others.

His severest critics often have been people who never wrote a recognized book, or whose books themselves are not without the flaws of typesetters and human errors, or whose dyspeptic nature made them discard a sculpture because of a chip.

The body of work produced by F. Stanley will become part of the vast lore about the Southwest. It will remain as long as libraries stand and will be consulted and used by generations as part of the grassroots literature. Future writers will correct its errors, just as their mistakes will be corrected by still later scholars. But someone had to start it, and F. Stanley was the man.

V

FACSIMILE OF NUMBER 290 OF THE
ORIGINAL 1958 EDITION

NO TEARS FOR
Black Jack Ketchum

NO TEARS FOR
Black Jack Ketchum

by

F. STANLEY

*Sincerely
F. Stanley*

Only 500 Copies printed
Of which this is copy

No. 290

Printed in the United States of America

WORLD PRESS, INC.
DENVER, COLORADO

Dedicated to the
Staff of the Museum Library at Santa Fe, N. M.
For their cooperation, help and time.

CHAPTERS

This is the life of Black Jack Ketchum who was executed for an attempt to hold up the C. & S. train between DesMoines and Folsom in the northeastern corner of New Mexico. His other daring deeds as a desperado were not considered by the court. Ketchum was to be made an example of in an effort to prevent further robberies as well as to prove to the rest of the nation that New Mexico knew how to deal with outlaws like Black Jack. Actually the hanging proved nothing. Rustlers, robbers, outlaws continued on their merry way. Few if any more trains were held up after the Folsom incident, but this was due more to the improved protective measures for baggage and express cars than any laws set down by the Territory; the speed of the new engines; the modernization of the railroad. With the dawn of the Twentieth Century any kind of hold-up became increasingly dangerous for the outlaw due to the progress of science, which proved to be the greatest lawman of all time.

I first learned of Black Jack when going through the Colfax County Court Records and the *Raton Range*. The Courthouse also stocked all copies of the *Clayton Enterprise* as well as the *Springer Stockman*. Here was a man whose misplaced bravery outshone the more widely known Billy the Kid. The boy wonder of the outlaw world looms as a Robin Hood, desperado, hero — depending on the one writing him up. He never came within range of Ketchum for daring, nerve, hard riding. He was a victim of circumstance; Ketchum wrote his own ticket. Both lost. Some people have made Billy the Kid and the Lincoln County War almost a religion. Too bad. After all, like Ketchum he was an outlaw. Began as a horse thief, in fact. It's the citizens that cry for law and order that build up Americana on desperadoes. While I plead guilty to this offense I also make an effort not to get fanciful and gush out sensationalism. The truth about men like Ketchum reads like fiction enough without distorting the facts or the need of embellishment.

I am grateful to Miss G. Hill, Ruth Rambo and the staff of the New Mexico Museum Library for help in research; to J. Yoakley whose father was a conductor on the C. & S. for many years and knew Frank Harrington intimately; to the staff of the Western Section of the Denver Library. No student of research does a complete job without frequent visits to this library. The people of Raton, Cimarron, Springer proved helpful, as did the librarians at the Freeman Building in Topeka; the librarian at Texas University, as well as the librarian of the Abilene Public Library. To all who helped, my sincere gratitude.

F. STANLEY.

Rotan, Texas, October 9, 1957.

NO TEARS FOR BLACK JACK KETCHUM

CHAPTER ONE

Friday 26, 1901. The turquoise New Mexico sky was cloudless. Off toward the horizon Rabbit Ear mound rose in starchy stiffness, a listening post on the bleak prairie, coned to an even bleaker sky. Little shoots were knifing through the adobe — crusted parched earth to form rather questionable green stalks, a harbinger of spring, a banquet for live stock, a relief to the rancher. The wind, as is customary this time of the year in northeastern New Mexico, was high and mighty. Now and then it spanked a whirl of dust and chased last fall's tumbleweed smack up against the barbed wire fence, to rest on the crest of last summer's sand. There was still a bit of frost in the air as winter attempted a few feeble, dying licks against the rapid march of the vernal season, causing the cattle to lower in animal patience. To the north Mount Capulin defied wind, dust, sound, as it shed its drab winter coat in favor of the hazy green. All about blew the sound and the fury, a babble of noises pounding out excitement.

This would be a day long remembered. The wind told the grass; the grass told the dust, and the dust blew it all over town. Wagons rolled into Clayton. From far and near they came-Santa Fe, Raton, Trinidad, Walsenburg, Capulin, Grenville. From all over the Territory. Spring-board, buck-board, chuck-wagon, Studebaker wagon, sur-rey, saddle-back, afoot. There were those who boarded the steam engine several days before so as to witness this event of tremendous import. Just about everybody from Folsom, too, was there, and Springer and Cimarron. Well,

1

they had a right. So they thought. It was near Folsom that the train robberies took place; it was in the area of Cimarron that many of the gunfights forced citizens to lock their doors at night; Springer telegraphed the strange events of this corner of the world to a Territory so mad at the daring of train robbers that it vowed to hang the first one caught. And the victim was Tom "Black Jack" Ketchum. Thus all roads lead to Clayton that Friday. The crowd was neither in a holiday mood nor were carriages draped for a funeral. Just curious. Most had seen a hanging before. Really it didn't matter who was being strung up. It was an excuse to delay the chores, butter the gossip, while away the time. One would readily admit that it was rather a singular event for it was a rather boring time of the year when one could hardly plant due to the uncertainty of a frost or a snowfall or a tornado. Now a hanging! Comes along like a traveling show now and then. You all look at the same thing but hide what you're really thinking. You say to your companion at your elbow: "Isn't it terrible." They agree. All of them—the companions at the elbows. Nobody walks away. Nobody explains why they came. The officers of the law don't have to explain. The editor of the *Raton Range* comments in his paper: "A large crowd of morbid humanity is congregated at Clayton to see today's grewsome spectacle." Nothing morbid about the expectancy on those faces. Weather-beaten, powder-beaten, just beaten, they came to see a show as some watch a movie or a congressman stumping for re-election. They have been milling around since dawn. The photographer looks at his camera, then at the scaffold. At the scaffold a few sheriff deputies are probing a board here and there like stage hands putting the last touches to the set before the drama begins. No one whispers. There is nothing to hide. And it is not a funeral. They are not talking above the wind. Just recounting the various deeds or misdeeds that eventuated in this day of days for Black Jack Ketchum.

2

No handkerchiefs are in evidence. Here and there the steel of Winchesters flash in the sunlight as they throw off the glare of the brilliant sun. Everybody knows that there have been rumors of an attempted rescue. Some of the crowd hopes for this: It will add to the excitement. No matter if a few dozen lose their lives in the attempt. Think of the screaming headlines. Who cares about screaming children. This same mob will go home this afternoon and call for the blood of a sadist somewhere afar off who brought gloom to the home of parents who but a short time before waved farewell to their little darling.

No doubt about it, Black Jack Ketchum is going to hang. You bet'chum. Sitting on the steps leading up to the platform, the reporters from the Denver papers watched the crowd. The wind, ever a gracious gossiper, carried snatches of conversation to them. Meaningless names whirled by. Persons, places, things. Palaver to the newsmen but not to the tall, heavy-set, pale prisoner adjusting the white tie against a white collar now that he seemed pleased with his black suit. His complexion had nothing to do with fear. He had been in prison too long.

The wind was from the south. Might help to bring rain. But not today. Here and there people rubbed their eyes as they cursed the dust that refused to stay on the unpaved streets. Now and then strands of last year's dry prairie grass blew against clothing. No one bothered to brush it away, not if they were from around the area— only city slickers. Inspecting the props were the reporters from Raton, Trinidad and Santa Fe. White, the photographer, bent as he spoke to a half grown boy at his side. Some day this lad would marry White's daughter and run the photography shop in Raton where tourists would stop to buy photos of the hanging and of the headless body under the scaffold.

The morning passed by uneventfully enough. The crowd already knew what the outlaw had for breakfast. They were quite satisfied that he slept well and were

3

convinced that he would walk the gang plank like a man
—without tears or story. That's the way they liked to see
a man die. The talk continued.

"Hear he's not nervous at all."

"Sure isn't. He's a calm one, that one."

"Shaved himself without a knick. As steady as you
please."

"See Frank Harrington made it."

"Don't guess he'd miss it for the world. Wants to
make sure Black Jack isn't going to shoot anybody else
before he dies."

"Heard tell Black Jack refused a drink to keep him
steady."

"Never took a drink in his life. So he said."

"Isn't that Captain Fort from Las Vegas testing the
rope?"

"Yep. Governor Otero asked him to come up and kind
of look after things."

"Looks like there are enough railroad men to do
that."

"The governor isn't taking any more chances than
the railroad."

Voices, like so many flies, buzzing. There were no
buzzards flying overhead. The people got there first. With
a show of vanity, as if conscious of his good looks, Ketchum dipped a large comb into the basin of water before
him and applied it to his jet black hair as he looked at
the Jesuit priest, through the mirror. He seemed so
pathetically small in his large frock coat. The condemned
man almost pitied him. He had come from Trinidad to
offer his consolation and to bring peace of soul to the
seemingly calm man so soon to make his last public appearance. Ketchum knew and the padre knew the turmoil
and strife within. Outwardly calm, Black Jack could joke
—with Thompson, Clark, Gracia, Fort, Harrington, even
the one man in all that crowd who knew that what Black
Jack needed above all at that moment was to unburden

4

his soul; take off the mask. Because he feared he would put up a front to the very end. He took the end of his big, black mustache and curled it; then the other side. He appreciated what the priest was saying but showed no sign that he was impressed. Nor did he order him out of the cell. They would go up the scaffold together—the little Jesuit from Trinidad and the tall outlaw from Texas. As the noose is pulled down over his head, just before the black cloth bag covers his face, the little padre, who only reaches to Black Jack's shoulder even with his stetson on, gives him one final look, whispers one final prayer. The dark eyes of the last of the notorious frontier train robbers rest for a moment on the man of God and the black bag descends. The crowd does not stand in awe. It's a hanging not a church. Pencils scratch pads as reporters work at the reason for their being there; White's camera has been clicking for some time now. Beside the stairway to the platform there is an additional ladder resting against the brick wall of the jail and the top of the platform. The scaffold is firmly built. It does not give an inch under the weight of the seven men standing on it. The crowd face these men; they face Black Jack; he faces eternity. Leave him there in the darkness under the glare of the noonday sun, the dance of the dust, the song of the wind, the hum of voices, the beck of eternity. Now is the time to ask, who was Black Jack Ketchum?

What did he think now that the black bag was in place? All during his imprisonment at Santa Fe he never abandoned hope that some of his former cronies would make a desperate attempt to liberate him. He had tried several schemes on the guards, doctors, attendants. They came to naught. The officials left nothing to chance. His left arm was chained to his side; his legs hobbled, nothing new to these men who had been tying horses' legs for years—a rope around his neck; a black sack over his head and likewise tied at the back, around his neck. This long, momentous span in the life of Black Jack Ketchum. There

5

are those who say that he was anxious for a dinner engagement in hell, since he had no dinner, and it was after one. There are enough witnesses to testify that he said so. But he would gladly postpone the junket in favor of liberty, should a few of his former comrades so change course of events. Whatever his obsession regarding his destination he wouldn't mind having the cards re-shuffled. All his life he had a complex about fire and brimstone. Possibly because it was a hidden fear and all the rest but sublimations. He must have grimaced at the crowd, under that black cloth—mocked, scorned and defied. That was Black Jack Ketchum. He might have even laughed at all the attention he was receiving. Two types of people have tremendous funerals after being hunted and persecuted in life—the saint because he plagued himself; the outlaw because he heckled society. With this scene set for the grand finale the flash back begins in Texas, the State of his birth.

It has been written that Tom Ketchum's father was a doctor. Harvey's District No. 2, northwest of San Saba in the county bearing that name, deep in the heart of Texas, would be the most unlikely place a medical man would be in the year 1866, when Tom was born, especially since the Civil War made many a Texan feel he had but little to come home to. Cattle ran wild, so did the Comanches. Homes were as pioneer-looking as they were meant to be. Women and children were thin, gaunt, sallow from several years hard labor forced upon them through lack of man power. A medical man would hardly select this local to put flesh on the bones of his children; bring happiness to their mother, especially when there was a crying need for doctors in every city in the nation. Richland creek, feeding the larger San Saba stream, flowed east and south. Here cattle could come to water; a man could try his luck at dry farming. And that is what Tom's father did. He might also make a little better living as a veterinarian, which accounts for his being called

6

doctor. No medical man, even in 1866, would call upon his children when they were scarcely able to ride, to hire themselves out to others for their bread and butter. No medical man would go off, miles from any settlement, isolate himself in Indian country, work on a ranch all day, struggling against Indians, drought, recalcitrant steers, digging rocks and roots in order to have a vegetable patch, leading a miserable existence, as if the war had not become history. A horse doctor, a man who treated animals, would not be out of place here where he was definitely needed. No one ever mentioned what kind of a doctor headed the Ketchum family because no one ever knew. Internal evidence, subsequent moves, all point to a man skilled in animal husbandry.

Richmond Springs was not even a community when Tom Ketchum was born. Here and there a small ranch house dotted the area, first settled but eleven years before when Jackson J. Brown scorned the threat of Indians, challenged the woe-begone looks of friends and put his hut in the valley. Others followed, among them the Ketchums. Tom was eleven years old before the government dignified the place with a post-office and that in the home of Sam E. Hays. No matter who moved in life was the same for all; watch for Indians, feed the milk cow, churn the butter, chop the wood, keep the fire burning, ride the range for strays, penetrate the live oaks for the hoary ones, see if your brand went visiting the neighbor's steers, look after the sick ones, feed the hogs, chickens, collect the eggs, target practice—and especially target practice. A man's life depended on his being a good shot. So did the lives of every member of his family. Tom was fortunate in having two older brothers, Berry and Sam, who could show him how to shoot. Also they pampered him. None of the three had any love for the drudgery of ranch life. Had it proved less of a chore almost from the cradle Sam and Tom might have died in the peace abiding obscurity that was the lot of Berry.

Years later when legends about Tom Ketchum began making the rounds as he languished in the Territorial pen at Santa Fe, the editor of the *Santa Fe New Mexican* came up with this bit of information: "It is related of Ketchum that, when only a boy roaming a west Texas ranch, in the enjoyment of all the freedom and boundless privileges of the original red man, he was summoned as a witness in a criminal case. He paid no attention to the summons, and from that time until one fateful night last month, when he attempted to rob a train alone and unaided, the strong arm of the law has been constantly reaching for him. The nature of the man is shown by the well authenticated story to the effect that, during his boyhood days on the ranch, one of his chief sources of pleasure was gained from a somewhat peculiar habit he had of hiding behind the chapparral on some lonely hill and from this vantage point shooting at—and seldom missing --the Mexican herders on the plains below. He has always upheld the reputation of nerve which he made early in his career, and his last exploit showed he was game to the backbone. He has never been known to 'quit,' as many a man who resisted him can testify, and as many more could testify if they were living now. He is in many ways a remarkable character, and had he applied his peculiar talents in other channels, he could have accomplished wonderful ends. As it is, it seems that he is doomed to take his last look at life through the bars of a prison cell, and he will not even have the satisfaction, so dear to men of his class, of dying with his boots on . . ." (Oct. 7, 1899 —quoted from the *El Paso Herald* by the editor of the Santa Fe Newspaper):

Tom Ketchum had very little formal education. He attended the Brown school house at the creek long enough to learn his letters; the balance of his education was from the school of hard knocks, the mesquite, the table land, cutting out cattle for the northern trails, listening to tales told by older and more experienced cowboys, hearing lots and lots of lectures at home on the evils of drink, paling around with his cousins and Duncans, envying the Harkeys, Halls and Browns their Indian experiences, doing odd jobs on various ranches while the men steered cattle north to the railheads. Thus he drifted from place to place an untamed, spoiled yearling full of promises made to himself, full of pranks and full of forebodings for the future. "The Duncan boys and the Ketchum boys were raised right at the mouth of Richland creek, on the San Saba river, and they got to be vicious criminals also. That was quite a settlement of farmers and small ranchers. Joe sent me up to the Duncans' place with a search warrant to search their premises for hobbles, bells, and harness. I notified as many of the neighbors as I could to be there in the morning that I was going to search the premises. There were quite a bunch of them there while I was searching the place. I finally found two flour barrels full of bells, harness, and hobbles, hid away in a smoke house. When I would ring one of these bells, some one of the old men would holler, 'That's mine!'. I arrested the two Duncan boys, Dick and Bige, and took them back and put them in jail..." Dee Harkey, MEAN AS HELL (p. 28). Every one of the Ketchum boys was a good hand, the experience having been acquired at the Hall and Tankersly ranches. There is a story told that Tom and a character named Bill Powers, but called "Jap" because he was sloe eyed, sat down to a game of cards at the little store in Richland Springs. Dame Fortune favored the younger Ketchum which brought forth some slurring and unfavorable comment from Powers. In the end, Powers lay on the floor dead and Ketchum high-tailed it for the Chisum ranch on the Pecos, in New Mexico. There was no courthouse within miles. Nor was there a Justice of the Peace. Even if there were the official would be persuaded that Tom acted in self-defense and the incident closed, which is probably what happened since no further reference is made to Ketchum's action until after his death. There was always excitement in the Pecos country and no doubt young Ketchum had his share of it. If he trailed any herds north he kept it very quiet, or he may not have stayed at Chisum's long enough to follow the herds to the rail heads.

Tom grew to be quite tall, handsome and slender. Bulk was to be added to his frame as he wiled away the months in jail. But he was a dashing, lanky, dark-eyed, black-haired, swathy-complexioned cowboy who was as adept at rustling, shooting and riding as he was at branding, shoe-ing, trailing. Both Sam and Berry admitted that Tom was the brains of the family. How much Berry helped in these early escapades is hard to say, if at all, for Governor Otero is to make Berry an unknown quantity later on. Concerning Sam there is no doubt. Whatever Berry's demerits, if any, prior to the Tom Green county days, he more than atoned for in his later efforts at making law abiding citizens of Samuel and Thomas. Harkey continues: "Tom Ketchum and Sam were indicted in our country for horse stealing. We located them in a little dugout in Cow Valley, in McCulloch county. Joe sent me after them. I took Jim Hall with me to help arrest them, but they broke out of this adobe house as we rode up, jumped on their horses and ran. They were both riding race horses, so I didn't try to race them down, but I arrested another fellow we caught in the dugout. I did not know who he was, but I took him to San Saba and put him in jail. I learned that he was wanted for murder at Temple, Texas, and the sheriff from Temple came and got him. Berry Ketchum, brother of Sam and Tom, moved to Green county and established a cow and horse ranch down on the Pecos river, where Sonora, Texas, is now. Tom and Sam made Berry's ranch their headquarters until they came to New Mexico in 1890. Then they went to work for L. F. D. Ranch, or the Littlefield Cattle Company, and we were never able to bring them back to San Saba for the stealing of horses . . . " (Harkey, o.c. p. 28)

10

It was the era of changes. The man that praised Richland Springs one year would be glorifying his new ranch around Lampasas or even as far north as Montana the next. Many factors were responsible not the least of which was the trend toward more railroads. The Ketchums were on the move along with many others, not as far perhaps, but still new territory. Twenty miles southwest of San Angelo, the Concho country, in Tom Green county, was the little hamlet with the surprisingly Yankee name of Knickerbocker. It was never destined for big things. Even now the Texas Guide Book fails to make mention of it. But the Ketchum family heard of it and located there. It was some time after this that Berry started his own place. Meantime the other two boys continued to work as cowboys, making friends, riding in and out of trouble from one outfit to another. Ben Kilpatrick, George Kilpatrick, Will Carver, Ed Bullion—they were better known to Sam than to Tom, this latter staying with Berry to help him locate his own place while Sam worked as a cowhand at the Tankersly place. After a time everybody in San Angelo came to know Sam, Ed, George and Ben. Will Carver was not as noisy as these. He presumed nothing and minded his manners. When they came in to hurrah the town of a Saturday night you would never suspect that Will Carver formed part of the group. Nothing rowdy about him. Polite, obliging, smiling, he ambled about with the air of a gentleman. They were nomads really, drifting from outfit to outfit gaining experience as they went along. They were often seen around the Mosely hotel in Pecos City and at the rodeo shows held there. The city attracted cowboys far and near as they came to pit their skill in competition. Rodeo was not a monomania with the Reeves county town; other allurements magnetized the steady flow. Pecos was a miniture Dodge as it was in its "end of track" and "trail driving days." To look at Dodge and Pecos today you would never imagine the gambling, wanton, wild, foolhardy, devil-may-care young

11

cowboys beating paths to the dens, saloons, dance halls, boot-hill. They never looked for excitement; they created it. Horses they were used to, shooting was child's play, drinking was a tonic, dancing was exercise but gambling was ever a witch, fascinating, captivating, possessing tantalizing, optative. It was the dance of death for Bullion, Ketchum, Carver, the Kilpatricks. None of them became robbers for the mere thrill of the hold-ups any more than for the possession of wealth. Money was the penicillum injected into their bloodstream to hypnotize as card followed card on the table which was no more than the game of chance that told the story of their own lives. From the number of their hold-ups they were as unlucky at cards as they were robbers. The fabulous sums they were supposed to have stolen has never been proven. They were to prove a later edition of the Sam Bass Gang.

Meantime Tom was not too far off. He separated from his brother Berry to go to the Seven Rivers country to complete his schooling as a ranch hand. This area was part of the terrain of New Mexico pretty well swallowed up by Texans. It was a wild, untamed country as osiose and addled as the roving cattle grazing the grass. The only sounds heard here were the shouts of cowboys and now and then the crack of pistols. There was just the land, the steers, the cowboys and the sky. Horizons were dreams to be shattered on payday. Here and there a sod house broke the monotony of the consonant earth. Somewhere out of reach beyond those barren plains was the growing trading post known as Roswell; to the south was Pecos City and Toyah where one found better comradeship and cheer than at Seven Rivers. Big Tom kept to himself out on the range but always sought the gaming table when in town. He was an uncertain quantity to the other hands because he had no love for liquor, cared less for dancing and never talked about girls. But he was a good shot. It wouldn't do to tease a good shot. The quiet, lonely type—no fun. What a waste of time to sit hours at a table trying to beat a professional gambler at his own game. He was a good hand. So were all the cowboys on the Chisum ranch and in the Seven Rivers country. Only good hands knew how to battle the elements, sickness, loneliness, antics of live stock, hidden dangers.

In the range country cattle were as recalcitrant as the cowboys. They drifted south with the winter storms as bison did before the days of the great slaughter. When the first blades of spring grass peeped out of the earth ranch foremen were in quest of good hands to accompany him in quest of straying livestock. The time of roundup was the romance of cowboying. Hands transferred from one outfit to another so that it was not strange to find Tom now with the Chisum outfit, then with the LFD boys near Roswell, or again in the Seven Rivers district, over to Toyah, Pecos City, San Angelo. Lots of outfits banded together for the roundup. Each camped with its own chuck wagon. A few had extra men riding alone, although Tom does not seem to have been one of these. Usually two men started from each camp headed in the direction outside of the range they wished to encircle. There they separated, taking opposite directions, circling the prairie until they met riders from other camps, all the while their loud cries went up and their pistols were fired so as to drive the cattle inward toward the invisible circle they cut out for them. The outside riders met, about faced on their circles in quest of trails leading off the range in the hopes of leading back any steers headed that way. At the camps other riders fanned out into smaller circles turning in the cattle even closer. The clouds of dust coming in all directions were not duststorms but cattle and horses headed for the roundup ground. Chuck wagons and remudas were always a welcome sight. Dinner over, the boys were on their mounts again hoping to pick up more of the brand they were after than so many others that had come a-visiting. However, they were polite enough to keep the cuts bunched together knowing that off on

13

other ranges other cowboys were doing the same for them. Thus with cutting horses, cow ponies, town horses, remuda spares, race horses, range horses, mustangs, and breeds good, bad and indifferent, Tom became a fairly good judge of horseflesh. He thought more of a good horse than a bad woman. During these formative years the pattern of life fell into line—gaming tables, horses, lonely nights under prairie skies, twinkling stars, soft-moving winds, the bray of cattle, the bay of wolves and coyotes, the swish of the tall, tall grass as the season flowered into summer, the roll of the tumbleweed that could cause a stampede, the smell of the coffee, bacon and the taste of the sourdough biscuit, the music of the jingles, the lullaby of the moving herd. He was not indifferent to all this. He never was. All his spare time, when not robbing trains or stores, not racing horses, not gambling, was to be used on the open range with the work he knew from childhood because here he was really free, really with his own as if he refused to recognize the possibility of a split personality that corraled him to the remuda of the bunkhouse or lassoed him to the haunts of men and the glitter of money reached by the tinsel of imagination. No woman was to take up the life of Thomas Ketchum as happened in the lives of Carver, Ben Kilpatrick, Doc Holliday and so many others; not for one iota. He was too fascinated with the open range, open game, open safe. Nor was it a question of piling up riches to bequeath his own old age pension. Time meant no more to Tom than the steers he rounded up. Nor did he know anymore where he was headed than the stock that bellowed their last hurrah at the packing house. Now and then he was able to relax at home, at Berry's place, San Angelo, the quasi-domicile of Sam and his buddies. The hunt during these carefree days was not for the end of the rainbow, the feel of fine clothes, the pounding hoof-beats of racing horse flesh; deer meat, trout from the streams, a cut of greasy bear meat, rabbit stew, were so

14

many inducements to satisfy the quest of happiness. They hunted, they ate, they fished, they talked, they separated and were cowboys again.

Mavericks the boys might have claimed and worked a spread of their own, seeing that Berry was doing so well in his own right. But Tom and Sam seemed weened on Maverick milk for all settling down would ever mean to them. San Angelo site of old Fort Concho, high center for the Chidester Stage, arrow of the California Trail, crossroad of the Goodnight-Loving Trail all so many memories before Bart De Witt dignified the place with the angelic name that perpetuated the memory of his Ursuline sister living in spiritual contentment at San Antonio. The not so spiritual trail drivers, soldiers, freighters, gamblers, painted ladies, bar tenders, rustlers, horse thieves quenched the well of loneliness in boisterous frolic that smoke-screened the respectability they dreamed about but never hoped to attain. Would San Angelo ever live down the Fighting Parson, Smoky Joe, Jake Golden, Monte Bill, Mystic Maud, the sheep wars, the fence cutting wars? Sam, Tom and the others were part of these fence cutting wars which accounts for their sense of values in cutting down men when they become phantoms of the robber trail. These range wars were in part responsible for the ease with which they killed messengers, baggage men, posse men who stood in the way of the loot they so desperately wanted. Those were the days when they rode about with good blankets, slickers, Stetson hats, saddles and guns.

Sam was as much a gambler at heart as Tom and proved it by opening a gaming table in one of the saloons at San Angelo. Carver was taken in as partner. The venture was short lived mostly because Carver refused to be tied down in-doors accustomed as he was to open spaces. Also he enjoyed his reputation as a wrangler of horses rather than of men. There is a suspicion that he was forced to retire because he sent a bully to boot-hill but that seems more of a legend rather than fact since the incident cannot be pin-pointed. Everybody tells about it but no one tells exactly when, why, where the shooting took place. A lame excuse is better than none so Carver is whisked away from what seems like a profitable thing, if not a good thing, to spend more time with Laura Bullion, the Kilpatrick Brothers and his own way of life.

During the years the Ketchum boys were growing up various causes contributed to the rise of the cattle baron who sought to corner the beef market as well as re-live the feudal splendor of tournament days, knighthood, shy maidens, crusading spirits, the devotion of the many, absolute rule, control of the masses. Ever since the close of the Civil War, English, Dutch and Scotch capitalists kept eyes across the Atlantic searching for investments. One of the major corporations launched in Scotland was the famous Prairie Cattle Company, Limited. John Guthrie Smith, Solicitors before the Supreme Court, Scotland, and an American named William A. Clark of Muscatine, Iowa, were trustees of the corporation known as the Prairie Cattle Company. A year after the formation of the company it began its campaign for empire that staggers the imagination. On September 7, 1882, the company bought live-stock and land and increased its normal capital to a half million pounds sterling in order to meet the demands of creditors. Three weeks later it issued further debentures to the tune of one hundred and twenty-five thousand pounds sterling. By the end of the year about 700,000 pounds sterling had been voted and raised by the company for investment in lands and cattle in the United States (See Colfax County Records, Raton, N. M.). Clark, a banker, associated with him another banker from Kansas City, by the name of Underwood. In making purchases the firm operated as Underwood, Clark & Co., which might be considered the American branch of the Scotch concern. During these early years the sky seemed to be the limit. It shouldn't seem strange that all the general managers of the Prairie Cattle Company were natives of England, with one exception. The purchase of a number of immense spreads in Colorado, New Mexico and Indian Territory was left to Underwood and Clark or to men they trusted.

The J. J. Ranch extended from the lower Arkansas Valley fifty miles east from La Junta and seventy miles south into New Mexico and Oklahoma (then called Indian Territory by some; Nations Territory by others; the Badlands by rustlers) embracing 2,240,000 acres. The foreman of the ranch around the Trinidad, Colorado, area was William Jeptha Todd who married Laura de Busk at Trinidad on January 1, 1884. This J. J. Ranch was part of the Prairie Cattle Company empire. Over in what is now Roberts and Hemphill counties in the Texas Panhandle old Hank Creswell owned the Bar CC (sometimes known as the Bar C) but sold to the Prairie Cattle Company. James McKenzie of Kansas City (not to be confused with Murdo McKenzie) was named manager of the newly acquired Bar CC.

When Tom Ketchum was six years old James, Nathan and William Hall drove a herd of cattle from Richland Springs to the lush grasses of the long Cimarron river about fifty miles north of the site of Clayton in what is now Union county, New Mexico, just south of Emory's Ranch, then a part of Colfax county. The Halls paid seven dollars a head and sold at fourteen dollars a head. Their brand was the Cross L. For ten years they improved the land and their stock. In 1881, W. R. Green came in from Trinidad to talk over the possibility of buying the Hall spread for the Prairie Cattle Company. That was the year the Halls branded seven thousand steers. The Halls sold to the PCC for $450,000. Moving north Underwood & Clark added the JJ brand to the Cross L. Next they acquired the Turkey Track, LX, LIT, and several minor outfits. By the time Tom Ketchum went to work there the Prairie Cattle Company had taken over millions of acres, a hundred thousand cattle, thousands of work and saddle horses. Bob Haley was the wagon boss, Al Ferguson was in charge of the chuck wagon, and was one of the best cooks the outfit ever had. Some of the other cowboys known to Ketchum were John Like, Grude Crow, John O'Dell, Jess Tanner, Arthur Ligitwood, Arch Lane. Tom worked under Green, Todd and Murdo McKenzie. His best days and longest consecutive period of service was under Todd. The Todds moved to Canadian, Texas in 1895. This is not the place to tell the complete story of the demise of the tremendous empire known as the Paririe Cattle Company, Limited. Toward the close of the century courthouse records list lines like these:

"This indenture, made in the year of Our Lord One Thousand Eight Hundred and Ninety-Three, between the Prairie Cattle Company, Limited, a corporation duly created and organized under the laws of Great Britain and doing business in the Territory of New Mexico in pursance of the laws of said Territory, party of the first part, and Charles Springer, of the county of Colfax and Territory of New Mexico, party of the second part: WITNESSETH, That the said party of the first part, in pursuance of a resolution of its Board of Directors, duly passed at a meeting at the office of the said Company in Edinburgh, Scotland ...., for and in consideration of the sum of Twenty Thousand Pounds Sterling, in hand paid by the said party of the second part, the receipt whereof is hereby confessed and acknowledged, hath granted, bargained and sold, aliened, released, conveyed and confirmed, and by these presents doth grant, bargain and sell, remise, release, convey and confirm unto the said party of the second part, his heirs and assigns forever, all the following described lots and parcels of land situate, lying and being in the counties of Colfax, Mora, and San Miguel in the Territory of New Mexico ...."

The miles and miles of buffalo grass, hazy blue lagoons in the spanse above and along ridges and horizons, the

18

mirages of sparkling water, here and there the little tent sticking up on the prairie, the cry of the coyote, the mixed breeds of cattle lowering along, following the leader; the sea of grass and the open country just now beginning to sing its swan song as fences begin to put in appearance. How well Tom knew all this country and watched its blood-red sunsets. There was a time too, when he hired out to the Sierra Grande Ranch Company which Stephen and Helen Dorsey transferred to Charles Springer according to the Colfax county court record reading: ''January 2, 1891 the Sierra Grande Ranch Company sold, assigned, transferred and conveyed to said Charles Springer all of its right, title and interest in and to that certain herd and brand of cattle known as the Triangle Dot herd and brand, said cattle having heir principal range in said county of Colfax; also all the horses in said Triangle Dot brand, and all the wagons, buckboards, harness, saddles, camp equipage, and all other personal property belonging to said company and used in connection with said herd.'' Tom was also to know the Bar EZ Brand of the Mountain Spring Cattle Company.

There was talk among the boys. Lots of talk and time for it on the open range. So many things were happening in this corner of New Mexico during these years he was a top hand. The Star Route mail scandal, coal deposits around Raton, the Maxwell Land Grant battles with squatters. He had seen and heard O. P. McMains on occasion and had made a number of trips to Raton, Cimarron and the Yankee country. If McMains proved correct there was no reason why he couldn't select the land he wanted despite the protests of the Maxwell Land Grant Company. No doubt that is why the Gang was later to camp at will in the Cimarron area. He learned that the Supreme Court favored the Grant; he saw the ordeal the anti-granters went through despite the fighting McMains and wondered if the land was worth all the suffering and ejections on the part of both parties. There under the blanket of the stars he lay awake nights pondering these many happenings, sounding out his own philosophy and religion, convincing himself more and more that there was no middle ground—just the good and the bad—those who followed the heavens and the others whose trend was everlastingly downward. His love for cards convinced him of his category. No one could tell him otherwise. He did his work well. Todd was always ready to recommend him. His was a roving spirit and the superintendent knew better than to keep him tied down.

The work was hard and the hours long. Tom decided to visit the folks at Knickerbocker, San Angelo, San Saba country, Seven Rivers, Pecos City, using up his hard earned pay at the various gaming tables. He was not a hard drinker and called for but few drinks if any. He himself testified in prison that he rarely if ever drank intoxicating liquors, which testimony differs from that of the writers who have him one foot on the brass rail, elbows on the bar, as jigger follows jigger down the old home stream. Time he spent in saloons—plenty of it—but that was because gaming tables were part of the furnishings. Neither Todd nor McKenzie ever saw Ketchum take a drink while working for the PCC. A game of cards he was ready to enjoy at the drop of a blanket. There are many legends as to how he came by the name Black Jack. Whether it was because of Black Jack Bill Christian, or because of Ketchum's own swarthy complexion due to exposure in the sun, or his fondness for the card game known as Black Jack, or his addiction for black clothes, while all are plausible and none proven the fact remains that he emerges eventually as Black Jack Ketchum who seems to be the leader of the Black Jack Gang in name only for many of the members have the habit of acting on their own and of mouthing off to the so-called leader. Of Black Jack Gangs in the Southwest there were many —consequently many crimes attributed to Tom's boys were actually the work of others. The Wild Bunch was not a branch of Ketchum's crew, although some of the boys in it at one or another associated with Black Jack. The legends are spreading about Black Jack as they did about the young rustler and horse thief known as Billy the Kid, who was never worth to the Territory of New Mexico, dead or alive, what was paid out for some of Black Jack's boys and for Ike Stockton's gang (many have used the spelling Stogden also). Like Billy the Kid, Black Jack had a number of unlawful incidents to his credit — or discredit — before Territorial attention was focused on him and the posters began making the rounds. In both cases it was the sheriff who had the final say—at Fort Summer in a bedroom; at Clayton, with a hatchet in cutting a rope. Black Jack was not a rustler but he was a horse thief, not for profit but because he was a good judge of horse flesh and wanted the fastest horses available for quick getaway. Why leave anything to chance? If a rancher had a horse that was nimble-footed, there was no reason why you couldn't just leave your apathetic steed and take off with the agile mount whose particular job was to outdistance the posse. Actually Ketchum was not a horse thief in the sense of trading him off for profit although the fact that he had a horse not his own and could show no bill of sale for it would be reason enough to dangle from a tree. Dangle he did. After a taste of lots of things not in the books, or, if in the books, against the law.

The rise of the cattle barons, the move of syndicates, the power of money, the feel of big spreads, the lure of horse-racing, the spell of the gaming table, the romance of being wanted even if by the law, the magic of sleeping as long as you want in the morning without being told what to do, and so many other things seen in saloons, on the range, in the city, in the hills, at home, at Berry's place, made one thing important—ready money and lots of it. Whatever the many paths to riches, the law of averages pointed to robbery, and the law of averages pointed

21

to the dead end and the gallows as the risk involved. He felt compelled by destiny. Just to be a good cow hand was not the kismet in which to round out his days. The alacrity of the work pleased him but it did not steady him. The clink of the coin and the flip of the cards were the bridesmaids to the greater love of the feel of money and the power to dispense it not for the common good nor even as a Robin Hood but for the satisfaction of one, Thomas E. Ketchum, esquire. He was like Coronado after the Seven Cities and he became as well traveled as the Spaniard before him. Colorado, Arizona, Texas, Indian Territory, Kansas, the Southwest—he knew it better than any pathfinder, abstractor, scout, hunter, Indian, gambler or traveler. With the aid of fast horses he was to create illusions that would make sheriffs jump out of their skins, even those south of the border. He was a terror, that commanding figure, with his dark good looks, his penetrating black eyes, his black hair, black mustache, black clothes, black abrupt manner in asking you to turn over your money.

Tom Ketchum came into an inheritance that amounted to well over a thousand dollars. Not a big sum for one who often saw more than that pass hands with the flip of a card but a most welcome sum to a man with a career in mind. The story of the inheritance is like most stories with men of the infamy of Ketchum and others of his class. Nobody knows just how the ball gets rolling, but it does. So no story is complete without telling about his inheritance. Does it mean that his father died? Perhaps since Berry and others are the one to go to Santa Fe, Clayton and elsewhere to identify Sam and Tom. If the father proved such a physician as some authors would have us believe, especially in San Angelo, would this be a likely sum for a medical man to leave his boy? His cattle and ranch would have brought in more as the family seems to have been fairly well off even in pre-railroad days.

Fifteen hundred dollars for all those years of blood, sweat and tears?

"James Ketchum had driven a herd from the San Saba and sold it in New Mexico (1867). He and his party had reached this point (at the head of the river) upon their return when the Indians jumped them. Thurston suspected from the sign—the moccasin tracks, an Indian stirrup and the many arrows about the place—that the attackers were Kickapoos. Ketchum's body 'bore evident signs of torture, being charred and blackened with smoke.' And yet strangely the men had not been scalped. Fragments of twenty-dollar bills from the sale of the herd were scattered over the battleground. The soldiers dug a grave ten feet long and six wide. From left to right they buried the Ketchum brothers, James and John, and companion cowboys, William Truman and Thomas Darnell, in the order named, and placed a small stone at their heads. They turned over the fragments of money to a cowboy from San Saba............" Haley, FORT CONCHO AND THE TEXAS FRONTIER, page 155).

These Ketchums seem to have been Tom's uncles. Tom himself was born just east of the town of San Saba a little over a year prior to this incident. This means that there were a number of relatives about who might have left the inheritance if it did not come from his own father. About this time Berry acts as the jefe or patriarch. He counsels, admonishes, pleads, advises, invites, preaches, offers land and cattle to the younger brothers in the hopes of squashing the wild oats out of their system. While Tom and Sam lend a helping hand they will have no part of the growing importance that is Berry Ketchum. What Tom thought of him he kept to himself for he rarely mentioned him; was aloof and distant when with him. This presents a family problem causing one to wonder since Sam is buried at Santa Fe and Tom's grave is a tourist attraction at Clayton. The family plot in Texas was not for them.

"One day Tom's oldest brother, Berry Ketchum, came to visit him (at the Territorial prison, Santa Fe) but Tom declined to see him. He said, 'Berry is my good brother. He is a Christian and belongs to the church. I will tell you how it all happened. He showed both Sam and me how to hold up a train. The three of us held up a train in Texas and secured about $100,000 in cash. Berry was the oldest, so he took the money and became a real Christian gentleman, and Sam and I had to rustle for a living. Once in a while, he would give us a horse and a few dollars, but, believe me, the dollars were very few. He has taught us just how to hold up trains and get the money, so we kept it up. He worried every time we visited him, fearing we might give him away, but we never did. No, I do not wish to see him.' Berry came over to see me and seemed to be a quiet and pleasant gentleman. He said that Sam and Tom were always wild and would not follow his advice to settle down and go farming. He said that he had promised to give each of them a good farm if they would work it, but they declined. Berry went back to the penitentiary and left some money with the warden to buy Tom what he wanted, such ah peanuts, candy, cakes and pies, as he was very fond of sweets. At the same time he asked the warden not to tell Tom what he had done. Berry returned to San Angelo without seeing his brother, but he visited Sam's grave and placed some flowers and a wreath on it. I felt sorry for Berry as he felt quite disappointed . . ." (Governor Otero, MY NINE YEARS AS GOVERNOR, p. 122.)

What prompted these remarks against Berry? Was it the bitterness of the realization that for both Sam and himself crime did not pay? There was Berry free as a bird building up his ranch by sheer determination, industry and labor, so successful in fact that he could afford to give a ranch to Sam and Tom. Perhaps it was the loss of the arm. With one hand he could hardly be expected to do a full day's work whether as a wrangler, cowboy or even hold-up man. No one fell for his acrimonious remarks about Berry possibly because virtue is its own reward. It is hard to imagine Tom who was pleasant enough with friends and often portrayed as a defender of women giving himself over to maliciousness and resentment as he awaited the hangman's rope. Especially against his older brother. As with Billy the Kid, Ketchum's first killing came about in defense of a woman. A cafe owner abused a waitress in language used with stubborn mules and (secretly) top sergeants. Tom asked him to apologize which he refused to do. In the fight that followed the proprietor was killed; Ketchum was wanted in Kansas for murder. While the legends balloon in time they speak well for Tom's healthy attitude regarding womankind. Because he is Black Jack Ketchum we say the incident may have happened. Sometime during 1894 cow punching days are over; the next five years create the legend of Black Jack Ketchum. Texas, New Mexico, Arizona, Mexico become his domain. Oklahoma, Kansas, Wyoming are doubtful. Because of the Wild Bunch and the Hole in the Wall outfit there are those who would like to believe that Ketchum controlled about everything from Wyoming to Arizona. There is no doubt that Tom was well known to Butch Cass dy (George Parker), Bob Lee, Harvey Logan, Loney Logan, Harry Longabaugh, George Curry, Camella Hanks and may have been with them in some of their hold-ups, horse-stealing operations and possibly rustling but he definitely was not linked with them in the matter of secret pass words, ritualistic hand sakes, initiations and other flights of fancy foreign to his make-up. If there was safety in numbers there was no secrecy. He gathered about him cowboys he knew and could trust. Will Carver, Ben Kilpatrick, George Kilpatrick, McGinnis, Franks and one or two others made up the gang.

The inheritance spent, Sam, Tom and Will Carver headed for the PCC outfit where Murdo McKenzie replaced Todd in calling signals. McKenzie who was later to idealize the Stonewall Valley near Trinidad, Colorado, as the most beautiful spot in the world. Here he built his summer cottage on the site of Weston's old log cabin. Here the alpine beauty was to know the smog of the Maxwell Land Grant War. While McKenzie was not as impressed with the trio as Hinkle, he had no reason to suspect their plans as hold-up men. Little jobs at first. A store here, a post office there, in out of the way places like Liberty near the site of Tucumcari, New Mexico, where Levi Herstein kept a grocery store. He was also postmaster and the object was to rob the mails. Instead of turning over money, he reached for a gun and Black Jack killed him. The place was looted; the money spent at Nogales in Arizona, then back to work again to throw everybody off the track. Tom did not hang around Clayton as many supposed for the very fact that no one at Clayton could identify him after the ill fated third attempt on the C. & S. railroad he was able to play along with an alias for several days until some one from Triniday was able to prove his true identity. Had he been the companionable sort of fellow some make him out to be about Folsom, Clayton, Raton and Emory Gap, his alias would not have proved so convincing even for those few days. During those first attempts the boys usually ended up on a ranch either for work or to study the remuda situation. Good, fast horses were an important factor in a fast getaway especially when the posse seemed as familiar with the terrain as the fugitives. While a great many of the crimes committed in Wyoming, Indian Territory, Oklahoma (While Oklahoma Territory was created March 2, 1890, the Kiowa, Comanche, Apache and Wichita reservations were not opened for settlement until July 1901 and were known as Indian or Nations Territory), Kansas, New Mexico, Mexico, Utah and Colorado were laid at the door of the Black Jack Gang during the latter half of the Nineties, many were the work of roving cowboys, lesser known Black Jack Gangs, the Wild Bunch,

26

Hole in Wall Gang, bandits from across the border, recalcitrant Indians on a holiday from their reservations, displaced railroad employees, and the horde of imitators of the Younger Brothers, the Dalton Boys, the James Boys. A number of these lesser lights preferred to be called "The Kid" or "Black Jack" as a study of outlaws in Colorado, Utah, Kansas, New Mexico and Arizona would reveal. Texas is left out of the picture because of these boys, at least in the Ketchum Gang originated in Texas and their loss to the Lone Star State proved a headache to whatever locality they chose to throw their saddle. An added attraction during these years is the more frequent use of dynamite. This is possibly explained by the fact that end of track men used so much of it coming through little lomas that stood in the path of rail placements. Many of the bandits of the Gay Nineties were experienced in the use of explosive because of their days with the railroad. Not a few cowboys were likewise experienced because of tearing up roots, rocks, obstructions for greener pastures especially in large outfits like the PCC where the breeding of finer stock and race horses was not unknown. Explosives were also used to open gaps for the flow of water, widen arroyos, foundations and other purposes. One of the Ketchum Gang was an experienced dynamiter. He was useful in opening safes in baggage and mail cars. Texas, as big as it was, became increasingly unsafe as a hiding place. While at least two hold-ups were perpetrated in Texas, the Gang knew better than to hole up there.

Stanton, Texas, once known as Grelton, is an old town in comparison to many throughout the plains country of Texas. On the Texas and Pacific Railroad, the early German settlers called it Mariensfield (Mary's Field). Barbed wire annoyed the C. C. Slaughter cowboys and caused lots of six-shooter activity about the place. Several years before Black Jack held up the train at Mariensfield the name was changed to Stanton to honor Edwin

27

M. Stanton, the Secretary of War known to all students of Civil War history. How much was lost to the railroad only Black Jack and the railroad knew. The sum varies with the telling as in the case of Sam Bass and the James boys. No more than several thousand dollars would be a conservative estimate. Hardly one hundred thousand. Such a sum no railroad would lose lying down. The T & P made very little noise over this robbery. The other hold-up was at Lozier, in southeastern Terrel county, not too far removed, as distances in Texas go, from the old camping ground of Pecos City. The surmise is that the ground work for this job was mapped out at Pecos. The haul here was good but the exact amount sheer guess work.

"Albuquerque, May 24, 1949—Has the disappearance of Col. Albert J. Fountain and his son, puzzling New Mexico for more than half a century, been solved? 'Sam Ketchum told me that his brother, Tom (Black Jack) Ketchum murdered Col. Fountain and his son,' says Bob Lewis, veteran Magdalena peace officer. Fountain was an adventurer-soldier turned lawyer. He and his nine year old son, Henry, disappeared January 30, 1896, near White Sands. They were returning home from a court session at Lincoln. Fountain's belongings were found scattered near his wrecked buckboard along the road. "Sam told me he was an eyewitness to the Fountain killings, Lewis said in an interview. 'There was a third man in the party, too,' he said, but he would not reveal his name. 'He told me (i.e. Sam to Bob) Black Jack wanted to get rid of Fountain because he had been too successful in prosecuting their outlaw friends.' 'I tried to persuade Black Jack not to kill the boy,' Sam Ketchum told Lewis 'but he said he wanted to destroy all evidence. I told him they would break all of our necks if they caught us, any-way............" (*Albuquerque Journal*).

It seems strange that Bob Lewis should wait all those years to present his story. One fortunate outcome was that in 1949 very few New Mexicans knew of the Foun-

28

tain case and cared less. However, for several years following the incident the case held the national spotlight. Oliver Milton Lee, Thomas B. Catron, Albert B. Fall and other political high pontiffs in the Territory were implicated, if only by induendos, in the murder of the long faced, long nosed, bigote-lipped lawyer who cut quite a figure in and about Las Cruces. Pat Garrett, Capt. Tom Branigan, Major W. Llewellyn would have enjoyed Lee's dangling from a rope but their testimony was too weak. The trial at Hillsboro brought out no more than what many already knew or suspected: That the lawyer and his son had been waylaid and apparently roughed up a bit before buried somewhere in the sand dunes of Alamogordo. The atomic bomb could not have set off a greater explosion. Col. J. Heman was foreman of the Lincoln county grand jury in 1896 at the time Col. Fountain secured indictments against certain people suspected of cattle rustling. Two of these were McNew and Lee. Ketchum's name never came up as a possible suspect during the trial because more than anything two political factions were at war and trying to incriminate each other rather than investigating the actual motive and rounding up all suspects. Although Sam Ketchum told Lewis about Tom and his motive for the double murders at the time Lee was brought to the witness stand Tom was very much alive. Lewis may have taken this into consideration before spilling the news. Even if he went to Hillsboro how could he prove Sam told him? Who would listen to him of all those lawyers, on opposite sides of the fence, trying to hang a man who wouldn't have hesitated to say he killed Fountain, if he did, but actually working against the symbol of the force they were trying desperately to down and kill. Lee was a brave man, a self made man, who had little fear for the slayer of Billy the Kid and was as contemptuous of him as he would have been of the Kid himself. The double murder remains an unsolved mystery. Black Jack probably attended the trial, taking his

29

sabbatical from the PCC ranges or the Maxwell Land Grant terrain where he had been in hiding pending his last hold-up which took place about three months after the trial. Many months had elapsed from the time of the disappearance of the lawyer and his little son to the day Lee stood up against his enemies at Hillsboro. If time should prove Ketchum guilty in this instance it will also prove that covering his tracks was an art with him. He might have disappeared into the night a mysterious figure that strange August night that embalmed his future. Tom says that his brother Berry started him off on his career of crime; Sam says that Tom killed the Fountains; who points a finger at Sam? Tom was not the type to go around killing people because of his friends. If Fountain had in mind prosecuting Tom or planned to implicate him in some way the reason for the murders would be obvious. On the other hand Fountain loved good horses and kept them in his corral. Could Black Jack have helped himself to a steed or two only to have them recognized by Fountain in his travels? Merely to kill the lawyer and his son because of friends is out of keeping with the character of Black Jack unless those friends had no choice save implicating him in their crimes. Speculation goes on at book length—Who killed Col. Fountain and his son? Was it really Black Jack Ketchum?

Duncan, Arizona, east of Lordsburg, New Mexico, is the State Highway checking station. It is also the marketing center for a farming district irrigated by the Gila river and a shopping point for cattle and ore. Lying in the Peloncillo mountains and a stop on Highway 70 it is hardly recognized as one of the toughest little towns of Territorial days. Today the population runs a little over a thousand but in the days Ketchum terrorized the community it was quite small. Here he held up the stage and the express office. Ashfork, known for its tinted sandstone, found today on famous Highway 66, was also the scene of the Resolute Mining Company hold-up. On the following day while this news was still hot the Gang held up the Hulaupi Mining Company office at Kingman about fifty miles (in a direct line by horseback but 112 by car on Highway 66) west of Ashfork in a country still sparsely populated. The four hold-up men seemed no more than four cowboys intent on buying new saddles. They got away with fourteen hundred dollars. Jake Bishop put up a fight and was stabbed to death. At least he was as heroic a storekeeper as Herstein depending on how you interpret discretion as the better part of valor especially if there is hope of seeing another day. Tom, Sam, Carver, Spindel and Cole Young held up the International Bank at Nogales and it is still a matter of dispute as to whether they got away with sixteen thousand dollars or were glad to get away with their lives. One hundred shots were fired during the three minute battle. Some shooting. No one was hurt. That there was an exchange of shots is convincing proof that bank officials must have been tipped off or were merely on the alert because of the many robberies committed in Arizona by the Black Jack Gang during July and August of 1896. Instead of heading for the Patagonia river or the Santa Cruz mountains in Mexico, Tom led his men several miles northwest of Nogales to hide away in the Calabasas hills, much to the discomforture of the sheriff of Pima county who resented a robbery in Santa Cruz county involving his best horse. The chase over, the four or five men made their way to Santa Cruz in Sonora where they hoped to hole up until the excitement died down. No one knows why they moved west to the Sierra San Jose to the Guadalupe range, up into Arizona again, to the Perdogosas, to the San Bernadine Valley to rest at the site of Germonimo's surrender. Skeleton Canyon, left of Apache (pop. 45) six miles on a dirt road, where Curly Bill and his men hid among the rocks and tangled chaparral to kill off a number of Mexican smugglers, Black Jack brought his men to a halt and there they pitched camp. Mexican authorities evidently

31

notified the sheriff of Cochise county for two days after Black Jack settled in the canyon a posse from Tombstone and another from Cochise (pop. 145) northwest of Skeleton Canyon bottled up the outlaws and called upon them to surrender.

Cochise was a station on the Southern Pacific Railroad. Exactly three weeks and two days after Ketchum's lone, unsuccessful attempt on the train that night near Folsom, two officers of the law among others got away with over ten thousand dollars. Five months later as Three-Fingered Jack lay dying form a bullet wound he confessed that one of the lawmen responsible for the Cochise stick-up was Burt Alvord. He was arrested and placed in the Tombstone jail. Freed by W. N. Stiles, deputy-constable of Pearce, Alvord escaped across the border. About twelve months later both Stiles and Alvord were again confined behind bars at Tombstone but dug their way to freedom. Alvord was seen years later in Panama. This was the Alvord who called upon Black Jack to surrender. Ketchum, knowing his man, merely mocked him and told him in no uncertain terms what would happen if an attempt was made to capture him or his men. Alvord returned to Tombstone for Sheriff Fly. This time Fly, Alvord, Hildreth and several others gave battle. None of Ketchum's men were hurt but Robson of the posse was taken back to be buried in Tombstone. The Gang roamed what is now Coronado National Forest. They made purchases at Paradise, Hilltop, Portal, San Simon but avoided all towns as much as possible even at the sacrifice of the gaming table. A week later they were at Wilcox, Arizona. Three weeks later Col. Young was killed in an attempted hold up at Rio Puerco, New Mexico. A U. S. Marshal on the train shot him as he concentrated on the train brakeman. This attempt on the part of Young (also known as Estes) may have been his own doing as he and Ketchum parted company shortly after the attempt on the Wilcox express office. There have been many instances where under-study's always feel that they know enough or are superior to the man from whom they are receiving their training until their first independent attempt proves how ridiculously wrong they were.

Thirteen miles south of Socorro, New Mexico is the town of San Antonio where Gus Hilton set up his store and rooming house to take care of the needs of the miners from Carthage, San Pedro, Antonio and the Chupadera range. His son became an international figure as a hotel man years later. Gus and little Conrad often rode to Carthage and even as far as White Oaks, northeast of Carrizozo. One day the Hiltons received news that the stage was held up in the Oscuras. This robbery was blamed on Black Jack and his Gang. As is usual in such cases the amount involved is not given. Northeast of Hachita and south of Lordsburg on present Highway 70 is the hamlet of Separ (pop. 44). Here the post office was held up and the gang escaped over Stein's Pass to the Dos Cabezas and the Chiricahuas, Sam Simon being their headquarters. They are sometimes referred to as the San Simon Gang. Today the population numbers seven hundred but it was smaller then and catered to the rougher element; not out of choice. South of San Simon beyond the hamlet of Paradise was Rustler Park, a gathering place for all sorts and conditions of men. Here they talked over their plans preparatory to the next foray. The battle with Sheriff Fly taught them the inadvisability of staying too long in one place as they quartered now at Cananea, now at Clifton, sometimes working as cowboys as instanced by Captain William French's experience with them at Alma, west of Mogollon in New Mexico, again at Robbers Roost near Hankersville at the junction of Muddy and Fremont rivers in Wayne county, Utah. This was the domain of the Wild Bunch and the Black Jack Gang was always welcome there. North to the San Rafael river and the Green River settlement (pop. 474) this whole stretch of eroded uplands, mesa-lined valleys, highlands, badlands, the locale of Barrier Canyon, Orange Cliffs, Horse Thief Pasture Meca. Here was Robbers Roost the refuge of wanted men. Entrance into the canyon is possible only at widely spaced intervals. Neither Butch Cassidy nor Black Jack Ketchum ever suspected that this was the inner sanctum of a pre-historic race, a natural for archaeology students where petroglyphs were silent observers of lawlessness. Hanksville (pop. 185) so isolated, so secluded from the haunts of men, the rendez-vous for the reckless breed whose only law was the six shooter. They ruled all the land south and east and were welcomed in the isolated spots because they had money to spend and because they preyed on the cattle barons. Turkey Canyon in the Cimarron country of New Mexico was not to come until later.

Back in New Mexico, south of the scene of the Separ robbery on present State Road 81 is the Machita community, headquarters at one time for the Diamond A outfit. To the east were the Cedar Mountains; on the west were the Playas; in between spread the Diamond A. Here they helped themselves to a change of horses, a few steers for food, a rest from prying eyes until Sheriff Channon rode in from Silver City to investigate their moves. They rode back into San Simon and Arizona one jump ahead of the posse. The November air was brisk, the sky clear, the scene peaceful until soiled and disturbed by the explosion of the safe in the post office. Bill Anderson (Broncho Bill Walters) was with Ketchum on this raid; He later died with his boots on at the Diamond A. The express office of the Southern Pacific at San Simon yielded nothing. The robbers back-tracked to what was once known at Barney's Station (Lordsburg) back over Stein's Pass to old Fort Bowie Spring, Playas de los Pimas, to Rustler Park and Sulphur Springs Valley near Apache Pass in Arizona, where Hays and Musgrove joined the outlaws. At Huachuca, southeast of Tombstone, Tom Ketchum and George Musgrove held up the express office and were almost tempted to shoot the railroad agent because of the small returns. The next attempt during that busy month of November 1896, was at Bowie (pop. 200) sixteen miles west of San Simon on present Highway 86, the town where Curly Bill and four of his outlaws once uncoupled a locomotive from a train and raced it back and forth, yelling, shooting off their pistols, pulling hard on the whistle cord, then, tiring of the fun backed the engine into the station. Ketchum's goal was the postoffice. It yielded very little. A hard riding crew, the next stop was Deming. This time it was a passenger train. Then back again across the pass into Arizona.

The Chiricahuas spread over forty-five hundred acres of multicolored monoliths transformed by erosion into gnarled figurines that seem to parade along the mountainside like marauders from some unearthly region. The pillars, cliffs, bluffs, solitary figures, gave rise to speculation even among the outlaws. Many of the formations and peaks had names: The Praying Padre, the Bishop, Ugly Duckling, Cathedral Rock, the Boxing Glove, Massai Point, Squaw Mountain, Totem Pole, Chinese Wall, the Mushroom, Sentinal Peak, Cochise Head and a number of others. Squaw Mountain is of interest for here Massai took the squaws he stole from the reservation and killed them. Here Sheriff Steve Birchfield cornered Black Jack and forced him to fight. The only casualty proved to be an outlaw accidently shot by one of the Gang. On the go again the fugitives camped in the valley between Stein's Pass and San Simon. Eight days later they were a number of miles southeast along the New Mexico Chihuahua border at Ojo del Perro just at the foot of the Sierra del Perro, today a little port of entry known as Antelope Wells. Ketchum, Hays, Musgrove, Will Carver who rejoined the Gang shortly after the running battle in the Chiricahuas, no sooner entered the territory than they were dogged by a posse. Surrounded, Ketchum decided to fight to a finish. It was Carver's unerring aim that caused the posse to give up the fight. Hays was killed and Musgrove wounded in the leg.

"Train robberies came into vogue among Arizona outlaws in the Nineties. Lonely deserts, convenient mountains, and trains bearing fortunes in their safes made the crime attractive. Train robberies at Canyon Diabolo, Maricopa, Rock Cut, Wilcox, and Stein's Pass were pioneer successes for daring spirits to emulate. Black Jack Ketchum was one of the most famous of these early-day robbers. After robbing a bank at Nogales, he killed a man of Sheriff Fly's pursuing posse at Skeleton Canyon, adding one more tragedy to the many tragedies of that famous pass in the Peloncillos. Black Jack, it was supposed, buried much of his loot in a cave in Wild Cat Canyon at the south end of the Chiricahuas near William Lutley's ranch. He called this cave Room Forty-four. Captured after a train robbery, Black Jack imparted to Leonard Alvorsen full directions as to how to lift this treasure. But, unfortunately, Alvorsen had no opportunity to go on a treasure hunt, being detained behind bars at Yuma. Falling heir to Alvorsen's information, Bert and Harry Macia of Tombstone ransacked Room Forty-four, but no doubloons or pieces-of-eight rewarded them . . . " (Burns —TOMBSTONE Page 229).

By this time they terrorized the whole country from the Continental Divide to Tombstone and from Springerville north to the border, and even further south in such towns as Cananea, Del Rio, Agua Prieta, Naco, Santa Cruz, Ascencion, Vado de Fusiles. The police south of the border were as much on the alert as the sheriffs in southeastern Arizona and southwestern New Mexico. Because many of the hold-ups involved postoffices or Federal property, troops were called to help with the hunt but they did little or nothing to halt the rash of agoraphobia instilled by these sudden raids. No town knew which would be next. If the sheriff entered one town Black Jack raided the one he just left. The soldiers from Fort Bayard

36

entered the field only because commanded to do so. The same held for the men from Fort Grant. The posses for the most part had ulterior motives—not that they would admit the fact to the newspapers that the most important thing about capturing the outlaws was the reward money. Most members of a posse did not ride for the thrill of the chase; the resulting bounty should success tend the effort more than compensated for the inconvenience or the exposure to bullets which was the chance they always took.

It is interesting to note that the Black Jack Gang never operated in large communities. An effort has been made to link them seriously with the Wild Bunch and the Hole in the Wall bandits. Individual outlaws from these Gangs were associated at one time or another with Black Jack but both crews were distinct from what is commonly known as the Black Jack Gang. At the end of November 1896, Black Jack decided to go into winter quarters. Several of the boys went their various ways, Sam and Tom, having sprouted beards either for the purposes of avoiding recognition or to protect their throats against the winter cold—a thing customary among cowboys—stopped late one night at the WS Ranch where Captain William French employed them as cowboys. Some time later they took leave of the ranch relieving the captain of several fine horses and one of his buggy team. This we know from his own book of recollections written some years later. The Ketchums visited Alma close by, the historic mining town often raided by Apaches and definitely detested by Victorio during the early days of its existence. Here Butch Cassidy operated a saloon and gaming table. While George Leroy Parker was his given name he enjoyed his reputation as Butch Cassidy. He was a cowboy turned horse thief. For this he was arrested in the spring of 1894 to January 1896 where he whiled away his time in the Laramie lock-up. Tom and Butch knew each other either slightly before 1896 or not at all. While Cassidy was looting Castlegate, Green River, Hanksville

37

and other places in Wyoming, Nevada, Utah, Colorado, Black Jack operated in Arizona and New Mexico. The two Gangs operated hundreds of miles apart. There seems to be no connection whatsoever save in the supposition that Sam and Tom wintered with Cassidy at Robbers Roost, where time was passed in playing cards, eating, sleeping, and awaiting the blossoming of spring. Once again posses were stirring, Pinkerton men riding, post masters edgey, baggage and express men wary, store keepers suspicious, rustlers active, horse thieves roaming the valleys, the Black Jack Gang had returned to Rustler Park, up over Stein's Pass, on to the village of Cliff (pop. 161), northwest of Silver City, and the chase was on again.

"A dispatch from Silver City, New Mexico, says that at 8 o'clock Monday night (March 22, 1897) two men supposed to be Black Jack and Anderson, held up Heather's store at Cliff, thirty miles from Silver City on the road to Mogollon. The postoffice and stage station were in the store. The robbers took $300 in money, rifled the postoffice for money, stamps and registered mail, took a gold watch, two new suits of clothes and two overcoats. They seized the stage horses and started toward Silver City." (*The BLACK RANGE,* Chloride, March 26, 1897).

"It is said that some of the Black Jack Gang has been secretly loitering about Deming, and the citizens of that berg have besmeared themselves with war paint and are holding themselves in readiness to give Jack and his followers a warm reception should they attempt to take the town. With such a gang of desperadoes at large over which the civil authorities have no control, it behooves the people of every town to be on their guard. Country postoffices and stores seem to be their chief objects of invasion. Indeed, it seems strange that the civil authorities of New Mexico do not make a stringent effort to run down this gang of bandits who have so long terrorized the people of southwestern New Mexico (Ibid. April 23, 1897).

38

About the time railroads began to infiltrate the Territory of New Mexico there was an old dirt road known as Cook's Emigrant Road that went from Horse Springs to Bear Spring to Sabinal, crossing water holes as it pointed northeast. It skirted the Sierra San Mateo and edged the Llano San Augustin (Plains of St. Augustine) where Al Clemens had a ranch. He kept a fine breed of horses. One night following the threat on Deming the Gang knocked at the door of the ranch house. Clemens himself opened the door. There were several crusty looking characters seeking admittance. Tom Ketchum did not ask, he commanded.

"We're putting up here overnight. Get your cook out of bed and rustle up a meal. We need fresh horses and plan to take them."

There was food on the table. Lots of it. Also six-shooters. Clemens had no choice. They ate the food as if not expecting another meal for a long time again or at least like half starved brutes.

"No doubt the posse will pass by this way in a few days. Right now they are on the wrong trail. When they get here tell them that the Black Jacks—yes, the Black Jacks, took your horses."

One of the men asked Tom if he deemed it advisable to leave Clemens alive to tell the posse. The majority were for killing the rancher and his cook. Leaving nothing to chance the men sat at the table all night keeping the cook and Clemens with them. At dawn three of them went out to round up the best horses. They thanked Clemens and rode off. By this time the Wanted Dead or Alive circulars really began to circulate and it seemed as if the area from Deming to Tombstone was really organizing to hunt down the outlaws. It was only when the going got too rough and people too serious about their capture that they finally decided to move considerably further east on the Maxwell Land Grant and in the Cimarron country. The first attempt on the Colorado & Southern was not planned in Turkey Canyon, but at the St. James Hotel in Cimarron. They requested the best rooms, demanded the best service, called for rare liquors, although Tom himself took none. All of this was paid for in twenty and fifty dollar gold pieces. They enjoyed gambling and tossed fifty dollar gold pieces about without bothering to estimate their losses. For many days at Cimarron they went to the old abandoned stone jail where they held target practice against its rear wall, with all the solemnity of conducting an experiment in science or a lecture in college. McGinnis, by far the best shot of the group, could drive a nail into a plank by shooting it in. He would swing a single-action Colt forty-five on the forefinger of each hand firing shot upon shot until a twenty-penny spike pierced its length into a tree trunk. Such a feat was possible to Clay Allison, Jim Courtright, Buffalo Bill, Wes Hardin and several others of six-shooter breed. Fred Lambert, illustrator, poet, rancher, ex-lawman, was in those days merely a juvenile bar-tender at the St. James. He found occasion to leave his father's hotel to watch these experts at work. It bothered him that a man like McGinnis should be so perfect with a gun but so imperfect as a citizen. He spoke to Tom Ketchum about it for it annoyed him considerably and, youngster though he was, he thought that McGinnis could be made to walk on the side of the law instead of leaving a trail of hold-ups.

"God made a number of things," Tom told him, "the earth, heaven and hell. The way I see it if He made one He had to make the others. But I guess nobody tells Him what to do. All the folks on earth will go to either heaven or hell. Now people like McGinnis and myself, well, I guess we are bound for hell. I know it seems strange, I will not go pleading for heaven if hell is where I belong."

One night they left the St. James. Shortly afterwards the C. & S. had its first robbery, September 3, 1897. Both the Ketchums seem to have been in on this one. Governor Otero covers the Folsom robberies in his book, MY NINE

YEARS AS GOVERNOR, Chapter Eight. "As I now (1940) remember, it was sometime late in the summer of 1897 that I learned that the Black Jack Ketchum Gang had established their rendezvous in a thickly wooded canyon in northern New Mexico on the east side of the Taos mountains in Colfax county not far from Elizabethtown and within sight of Old Baldy. (Actually this rendezvous was not to come until the time of the second hold-up) Learning this about two months after I became governor, I at once notified the sheriffs of Colfax and Taos counties to keep a close watch on the gang and to notify me promptly should they make any attempt to move. I learned that besides Tom and Sam Ketchum, the Gang consisted of Will Carver, alias G. W. Franks, whose real name I believed to be Harvey Logan; William Walker, alias Broncho Bill; and Ezra Lay alias William H. McGinnis. All five of these men were at their headquarters. Will Franks was a wonderful shot with either rifle or pistol, and was regarded as the most desperate man in the bunch. He was a plausible sort of fellow, a good mixer and a good talker, so he usually did the scouting for the party, and located the 'easy money'. Clayton, the county seat of Union county, was a comparatively new town and the headquarters for cattle, horse and sheep men. In those early days it was overrun with gambling houses, saloons, dance halls, houses of prostitution, and rustlers. Much ready cash was in evidence, and the Colorado and Southern Railroad brought it in to Clayton from Colorado points almost daily. Franks soon learned all the facts and located the best point on the railroad right-of-way for a hold-up, which was five miles south of Folsom near Twin Mountain. After acquainting himself with all the details, he mounted his horse and struck the trail for headquarters. He soon made known his plans to the Gang and Tom Ketchum said, 'We will try it. Let's waste no time, but get ready at once.' As soon as arrangements were made, Broncho Bill was left in charge of the 'Robbers Roost' and the others left on good horses in the direction of Folsom. On the night of September 3, 1897, the south-bound passenger train of the C. & S. Railroad entered New Mexico through Emory Gap, without mishap. The engineer was Crowfoot, the fireman Crackley, and the conductor Frank Harrington. The train stopped for a few minutes in Folsom. As it started south, a man jumped on the front end of the express car to the engine, and quickly climbed over on the tender. At Twin Mountain, where there is a slight grade, the man dropped from the tender into the engine's cab, where he covered the engineer and fireman with his rifle. 'Stop the train,' he yelled to Crowfoot. Finding himself looking into the barrel of a rifle, the engineer quickly complied with the order. When the train came to a stop, the engineer and fireman were ordered to jump off and line up. The strange visitor was none other than Black Jack and the three men walked back to the door of the express car where Crackley called out to the express messenger to open the door, which he did. At this point, Black Jack was joined by Sam, his brother, and Will Franks. The other member of the Gang, McGinnis, was left to guard the four horses. Crowfoot, Crackley, and the two Ketchum boys climed into the express car, while Franks stood guard at the door. 'Open the safe,' commanded Black Jack. 'I can't,' said Drew, 'It is a through safe, and I don't have the combination. 'You lie,' said Sam, striking Drew over the head with his rifle. The latter fell to the floor, stunned by the blow. 'Hand up those sticks,' said Black Jack to Franks. Several sticks of dynamite were passed to him and five of them were placed on top of the safe. Throwing a quarter of fresh beef on top of the sticks, he lighted the fuse and the men stepped back. The explosion broke open the safe door and damaged the roof of the car. While the Ketchums were in the express car, Harrington came up from the foreward passenger coach toward the disconnected express car, swinging his lantern. Franks called out, 'Go back where you came from and put out that light before I shoot it out.' A sack holding silver dollars had been torn open by the explosion and the contents were scattered over the car floor. Sam Ketchum, however, picked the silver up and made the sack secure. 'Now get back to your engine,' said Black Jack to the engineer and fireman, 'and continue your journey south.' On their arrival in Clayton, Harrington reported the robbery. Immediately after the robbery, which took about thirty minutes, the bandits mounted their horses and rode off towards their rendezvous in the Taos mountains.

"Dixon, the rear brakeman, jumped off the rear Pullman and hurried back to Folsom to report the robbery. Posses were organized in Trinidad, Clayton and Folsom. The next morning they visited the scene of the hold-up, but the bandits had disappeared. The booty secured on this first hold-up was reported to have been $3,500............"
(Otero- o.c. pp. 111-112-113).

Through the mountains by easy stages, sleeping by day, traveling for the most part at night, the Gang was back in Rustler's Park in the Chiricahuas. It would seem foolish for them to hide in the Taos Mountains since, as Gov. Otero says, their rendevouz was an open secret. How can you imagine men as experienced as they in out-witting posses deciding to hole up in a place known to every one in Cimarron, Springer, Raton, Maxwell City and half the people of Santa Fe? The sheriffs of Colfax and Taos counties must have done some tall explaining to the Territorial governor especially since he cautioned them to be vigilant and to notify him the moment they noticed the outlaws went ariding. Somebody was asleep on the job. The outlaws not only gave them the slip but leisurely robbed a train in the bargain. As the story of this first robbery spread in the telling, by the time it made the rounds, all the passengers were relieved of their money before Black Jack decided to vanish in the darkness. Nobody ever gives the same version of crimes committed by

43

outlaws anymore than you will find only one version of the life of Shakespeare, Robert Burns, Napoleon, Caesar. Even the Gospel message has come to us in four versions and a number of epistles. No doubt the posses looked over the situation at Turkey Canyon following the hold-up and found nothing. There is no reason to believe that they had a hide-out at the place at all prior to the second attempt on the train. Why target practice in Cimarron if they had a camp in the canyon? Why the weeks at the St. James? The answer is that the robberies are confused and often many writers giving the account of Ketchum's activities are totally in ignorance of the incident of September 3, 1897. Very little is heard from Black Jack until December.

"News has been received here (Silver City) of a desperate fight that recently occurred near the border of Arizona and Old Mexico. According to the report, three guards of the Mexican service and one desperado were killed. The desperado was Frank O'Phallard, one of Black Jack's Gang, and an outlaw from Texas. The border guards learned of a raid designed by Black Jack to loot a town (Del Rio on the south bank of the river between Verde and Cananea in Old Mexico) across the river. A start was made from Leander Springs (old San Pedro Springs near the border in Arizona) and the guards had no difficulty in finding the Gang. The forces met face to face at a turn in the road. There were eight outlaws against three officers, but the latter opened the attack with orders for 'Hands up!'. Two outlaws turned their horses for the hills, but O'Phallard dismounted and drawing his Winchester opened fire and killed the three officers before he fell with a wound in his side which proved fatal. In his pocket was a letter from Miss Edith Cunningham, of Las Vegas, stating that her brother had just been shot and killed by Duck Manley at Red River, New Mexico. O'Phallard (also spelt Phallard) is the last of the Sam Bass Gang of train robbers who cleaned out the custom house at El Paso many years ago. His two broth-

44

ers were killed in the Panhandle of Texas by State Rangers." (Quoted in the *SANTA FE DAILY NEW MEXICAN* as a dispatch from Silver City December 10, 1897)

Biographers of Sam Bass fail to mention the incident at the El Paso custom house and the name O'Phallard either because this Gang was not responsible for the robbery or overlooked it in the light of the Bass exploits in East Texas. Many times cowboys would latch on to men like Bass, Cassidy, Ketchum for one incident in which they played a very minor role then brag about it later in the hopes of widening their reputation as gun slingers, desperadoes and thoroughly bad hombres. Despite the fact that he rode with Black Jack and outside the pale of the law there is no question of his bravery. The ones that made for the hills may have believed that descretion is the better part of valor but they must have felt sheepish in seeing one man take care of the three pursuers. The three lawmen probably never received posthumous medals or even a decent Christian burial but there is no doubting that they meant business in meeting the Gang face to face and challenging them to surrender despite the fact that they were outnumbered almost three to one. A law enforcement man had to have as much guts as an outlaw. Actually, the fight took place on the 5th of December although the press did not report it until five days later. One reason for this was the scarcity of dailies both in Arizona and New Mexico. Most of the papers of both Territories were weeklies; by the time the exchanges reached Santa Fe or Albuqureque the news was several days old. In those days the expression as old as yesterday's newspaper did not hold. News was news no matter when it reached the public due to the scarcity of libraries, books and reading material in general, also due to a lack of schools. On September 9th came the unsuccessful attempt at Stein's Pass.

"Last night the Sunset Limited had just left Stein's Pass, New Mexico, near the Arizona line, when the engineer noticed a danger signal and immediately applied the air brakes. No sooner was the train stopped than five men stepped out from their hiding places. One of the men covered the engineer and fireman with a Winchester while others gave their attention to the train proper, more especially the express car, firing guns in the air and otherwise frightening the passengers. At this point the guards in the express car took a hand in the fusillade. Thirty or forty shots were fired by both sides. One of the Wells Fargo guards, Jennings, succeeded in killing Edward Cullen, who was nearest to his car, and who was evidently the leader, for as soon as the other robbers noticed his body lying on the ground they made a break for their horses. No express money was stolen and no passengers were hurt. Jennings is a mere youth, a little bit of a fellow and used to work in Las Vegas for the Wells Fargo Company. He is well known in New Mexico.'' (Ibid. December 10, 1897 quoting a dispatch from El Paso, Texas)

''U. S. Marshal Forsaker returned from the southern part of the Territory on Saturday night where he had been for a number of days superintending the hunt for train robbers, and to a representative of the New Mexican (newspaper) he gave the following account of the attempted train hold-up at Stein's Pass last Thursday night:

''On Tuesday night of last week Mr. Forsaker left Deming with a car load of horses and went to Bowie, Arizona Territory, on the Southern Pacific, where he was met by sixteen picked men from New Mexico and Arizona. The men took the animals and a camping outfit, and, going to the mountains established a camp about twenty miles east of Stein's Pass. It was known that the desperadoes were in that vicinity, and the place selected for camping was a good one from which to watch their movements and to start after them as soon as their whereabouts were actually known. That another raid on trains

46

was contemplated by the robbers was not known, and the object of camping where they did was to keep watch on the Gang. The men in camp reported that on Thursday night from dark until about one o'clock signals of fire were seen in the mountains to the west at intervals of about fifteen minutes, but they could gather nothing from them.

"Marshall Forsaker remained at Bowie awaiting developments, and on Thursday night received a telegram from Stein's Pass telling of the attempted robbery. He at once started a messenger on horseback to the camp, instructing the men to meet him at a certain point on the railroad, with their horses. He then secured an engine and one car and went to the place named, where with the help of the trainmen, a chute for loading the horses was built. By the time these preparations were completed, eight of the sixteen men arrived, and, in an hour and a half after the train was stopped (by the robbers) the posse was at Stein's Pass. On reaching that little station it was learned that five men had made a raid on the place, securing about two dollars at the postoffice, twenty-five cents at the express office and relieving the station agent of about ten dollars. The express messenger, and a guard named Jennings, opened fire on the desperadoes killing one and wounding another. The resistence offered by these two brave men drove the Gang away and the train proceeded west. The eight men who remained at the camp, at break of day started out, and soon struck the trail of six horses which, so far as it is known they are still following. On Friday afternoon they picked up two horses, one of which had on a saddle.

"There is no further question but this Gang is the one that held up the Santa Fe train at Grant's Station a short time ago, and had remained in the mountains of southwestern Grants county for the purposes of making another haul before leaving the country. Mr. Forsaker is pretty well satisfied that the sixteen men on the trail will give a good account of themselves in a very short time. The trail was new when found; the horses fresh and in good condition, and everything is favorable to the overtaking and apprehension of the bandits and rustlers who have terrorized southern New Mexico for several years past.'' (Ibid. Dec. 13, 1897)

"News has been received here (at Silver City which sent the dispatch to Santa Fe) that a special Wells Fargo officer, J. N. Thacker, assisted by a posse of deputy U. S. Marshalls under Cipriano Baca, last night captured the entire Gang of train robbers, who, on last Thursday held up the Southern Pacific train at Stein's Pass, in the fight incident to which, one of the robbers was killed. At the time of the hold-up, the posse which had been anticipating an attack, was congregated at Bowie about thirty-five miles from Stein's Pass. The trail of the robbers was immediately taken and late last night the five remaining members of the Gang were surrounded in a cabin at the Cushey Ranch, about twenty-five miles this side of the Mexican line, in eastern Arizona. The robbers were taken completely by surprise and surrendered without a single shot being fired. Their names have not yet been ascertained, but they are cowboys who have been working in the vicinity of San Simon valley and have no connection with the notorious Black Jack Gang of border bandits. They have been brought here to await trial. When captured the robbers were endeavoring to escape across the line into Mexico.'' (Ibid. December 14, 1897)

The prisoners were Leonard Alverson, Dave Atkins and Edward Cullen. These were sentenced to the Territorial Penitentiary at Santa Fe. Before his death Tom Ketchum confessed to the robbery at Stein's Pass and asked that the three innocent victims be released. The five bandits implicated in the attempt at Stein's Pas were Tom and Sam Ketchum, William Carver, Ed Bullion, Broncho Bill. The one killed by Jennings was Ed Bullion. Tom was particularly anxious not to leave this life knowing that others were suffering for the crimes he committed, or he may even have been pained to know he was not credited with the Stein's Pass hold-up. Despite posses closing in on them the desperadoes held their ground and remained in the area as we learn from a dispatch from Tucson dated January 19, 1898: "It is reported that Black Jack's Gang was surrounded in the mountains near the boundary line by several posses, including a posse sent out by the Mexican Government, and a fight occurred in which one robber was killed and four captured. Two attempted to escape and were shot in their flight, the other two were in the hands of the Mexican officers, and it is claimed met death in like manner. The remainder of the free-booters went into a southerly direction and are supposedly in the Sierre Madre Mountains . . ."

During most of 1898 the Gang worked as cowboys for the evident reason that too many posses were in the field and too many detectives were watching the places the Ketchum boys were known to visit. It has been said that the hold-up at Lozier Creek and at Stanton occurred during this year. The brothers were known to have visited Llano, Lockhart and other places in Texas during this year. They may even have hazarded a visit to San Angelo and other places they knew as children. Coleman, the county seat of the county by that name, is on the Santa Fe Railroad. It is interesting to note that Coleman is not far from Richland Springs. On the night of June 9, 1898, the train was held up on its run from Brownwood to San Angelo. While Jeff Taylor, Bill Taylor, Pearce Keaton and Bud Newman were implicated, newspapers later brought in the names of Tom and Sam Ketchum as part of the band that pulled the Coleman hold-up. They said that the Ketchums returned to Arizona to escape Texas officials hunting the robbers especially since Fireman Johnson died at Santa Anna as a result of wounds received in the Coleman raid. When the Taylor brothers were eventually captured at their own ranch they were given ninety-nine years each at Huntsville because of the death of Johnson. One of the brothers managed to escape the Brown county jail where he awaited transportation to the State penitentiary. He was captured and escaped a second time. There seems to be no explanation as to why the papers linked the Ketchum boys with this Coleman hold-up except to have a plausible reason for the presence of Tom and his followers in Arizona once again. Several of the boys worked on Captain French's ranch. The Ketchum brothers worked on ranches about the mining camp of Kingston, American Valley, Lake Valley, Hillsboro, ever on the move, always avoiding towns because of the posters showing Black Jack facing and in profile, and wanted dead or alive. Even Billy the Kid was not as hunted as Black Jack nor as valuable dead or alive. The Kid represents more of a challenge because so little is really known about him. Had it not been for the fascination the Lincoln County War holds for some, the Kid would have died as he lived, an inconspicuous horse thief. Because the passage of years brings dimension in retrospect he stimulates research and ceases to be a reality but a legend like Robin Hood and others whose deeds multiply with the years until they are above reproach and beyond recognition as to their true characters. It would be interesting to watch the reactions of people who make a cult of Billy the Kid, if, living in his time they were told he killed their father or brother. The way he is glorified it seems that Pat Garrett is the one that should have been hung and Governor Wallace shot for putting a price on his head. With certain individuals he has become an obsession and a disease. With Black Jack Ketchum only time will tell. By July 1899, the Gang was united again. Tom does not appear in this second attempt on the C. & S. Lots of explanations have been offered but nobody knows, nor shall they ever know any more than they can ever know the childhood of Billy the Kid.

Chapter Two

"Late in the spring of 1899, the Gang had a falling out with their old leader, Black Jack. Sam Ketchum was delegated to inform his brother of their determination to quit him. Sam had decided to go with the Gang, and early one morning Franks and Broncho Bill gathered up their belongings, mounted their horses, and rode north. This time they located their headquarters on Turkey creek, in the canyon ten miles above the town of Cimarron, where they had several horses and a good supply of grub and ammunition. Franks scouted around for awhile and finally decided it was about time to attempt a second hold-up at Twin Mountain. Since the other bandits readily assented to the suggestion, preparations were in order. At this point, Broncho Bill decided to leave the bunch, so he told Sam Ketchum that he was disgusted with camp life and declined to stay in the camp during their absence. They cached their camp outfit, and the remaining three mounted their horses and soon reached their destination between Folsom and Twin Mountain.

"On July 11, 1899, the Gang again held up the south-bound passenger train at the same spot where the first hold-up had taken place. Frank Harrington was again the conductor, engineer Tubbs was in the cab, and Homel Scott was in charge of the express car, which carried considerable money. As the train rounded the curve at Twin Mountain, Tubbs noticed a fire on the prairie ahead of his train. 'Some sheepherder's camp,' he told his foreman. When the engine reached the fire, an uninvited guest with a pistol in each hand entered the cab from the tender. 'Stop her,' he ordered. The engineer promptly shut off the steam, and the train stopped within three hundred yards of the scene of the first hold-up. The stranger, who was Franks, forced the engineer and fireman to walk to the express car where he was joined by Ketchum and McGinnis. They fired a few shots to frighten the passengers and prevent their interference. The noise of these shots, however, informed the alert express messenger, Scott, that something unusual was happening. Accordingly, he hurriedly seized several packages of currency from one of the safes and threw them among a pile of merchandise and fruit boxes, where the robbers failed to find them. A second safe was blown open with dynamite, and the bandits jumped out of the car with the loot, which I am told, amounted to $70,000. The three bandits then crossed the track and made for their horses.

"Meanwhile, Conductor Harrington had realized that another hold-up was under way. Having secured a gun from a closet in the smoking car, he enlisted the assistance of two deputy sheriffs who happened to be on the train. The three men went through the train to the rear Pullman, and dropped to the ground. Seeing a bunch of horses by the light of the fire, they crawled toward them in the hope of preventing the escape of the robbers. Their share in the adventure being unknown to the engineer, the latter blew his whistle, and started the train without them. As it turned out, the conductor and the two deputy sheriffs were too late. The bandits secured the horses and rode off in the direction of Turkey Canyon . . . " (Otero o.c. page 113-115).

"Southbound passenger train No. 1 on the Colorado & Southern railway was robbed by four men five miles south of Folsom, New Mexico at 10:30 last night at the same point the hold-up occurred last September. They blew open the express car with dynamite and went through the safe, but the express messenger says there was nothing of value in it. Others say it contained a large

52

amount of money. Passengers and mails were not molested ....'' (From Trinidad, Colo, as quoted in the *SANTA FE NEW MEXICAN* for July 12, 1899)

"Yesterday afternoon U. S. Marshal Forsaker's posse of five men, with Sheriff Farr, of Huerfano county (Walsenburg) Colorado and W. H. Reno, special agent of the Colorado Southern Railroad struck the trail of the C. & S. train robbers near Cimarron, twenty-three miles west of here. They followed the trail into the mountains for a distance of about ten miles, and came upon the bandits when they were preparing to camp about 5:15. A demand for surrender was made, which was refused, and a fight ensued, in which about fifty shots were exchanged.

"There were three in the robbers band, all mounted. The marshall's posse was made up of F. H. Smith of New York, who was at Cimarron and volunteered to go with the party; H. M. Love, an employee of Charles Springer; J. H. Morgan and Perfecto Cordova of this county, with Sheriff Farr and special officer Reno. Farr was shot first through the wrist and having bandaged his wound renewed the battle. Next Smith was shot through the leg. Farr was again shot through the body and fell dead. Love was shot through the thigh and is in a dangerous condition. The firing lasted about forty-five minutes. The officers claim that one man of the robbers was killed and another wounded and they have a certainty of getting a third man. Mr. Reno remained on the ground until 8 p.m. and then went to Cimarron to summon a physician but owing to the rain and darkness did not reach there until midnight when he telephoned here (Springer) and Doctor Hines started for the scene. The officers claim to know all of the robbers but will not tell. It is said however that one of them is a man well known here, who was indicted for train robbery about the same place some time ago ... The body of the train robber killed was found and brought to Cimarron. He is a man six feet, two inches tall and weighs about two hundred pounds, light complexion. The

robber killed is known by the name of Wm. McGinnis and
also G. W. Franks. He is from Magdalena, New Mexico
and was a bronco buster. The body will be brought here
(i.e. to Springer) this evening when an inquest will be
held. The other two robbers abandoned their horses and
took to the hills. A posse of twenty men are hunting them.
Captain Thacker, special agent of the Wells, Fargo, Co.
is here attending the express company's end of the business.'' (*SANTA FE NEW MEXICAN* for July 17, 1899
quoting dispatches from Springer)

This was the news as it was first received. Without
stopping to investigate, the telegraph office sent the statements to Santa Fe and the rest of the Territory. This accounts for the many conflicting statements found in various authors covering the story of the death of the sheriff
from Colorado. Black Jack was working on a ranch in an
isolated area where he had no occasion to see a newspaper
and his brother Sam was dead and buried before all this
excitement became news to him. The posse was composed
of six men. Ed Farr had charge of three and Forsaker
had the other three. They decided that by coming upon the
camp in opposite directions they could take the desperadoes by surprise. Several factors would make this hard
going. One which is often overlooked was the heavy downpour, the lightning and thunder and mud. The rain was
the best ally the bandits had.

''The body of the robber was not found as was first
reported. Only one man was killed: Sheriff Farr. His
body has been taken to Colorado. Deputy Marshall Love
was wounded by a bullet striking a large pocket knife
and driving it through the leg near the hip. Joe Smith
was wounded through the fleshy part of the calf of the
left leg. . . . The camp of the outlaws seems to have
been used for two months. One dead horse was found
there and another wounded one. This latter was killed by
the posse. McGinnis is believed to be killed or at least
wounded. The body has not been found. Smith was the

54

first to fall. He was a friend of Garrett & McCormick and was staying at their ranch in Cimarron. He is a young man. Reno had two bullet holes through his coat, a ball through his trousers grazing the leg at the lower left side. Farr was born in Kerrville, Texas, thirty-five years ago (1864) and came to Huerfano county in Colorado in 1881. He married in 1895. He had been sheriff three years at the time of his death. He and his brother shared extensive cattle interests. Before coming to Colorado, in 1879 he was foreman of the McCartney ranch in San Miguel county, New Mexico. He left a widow and two children. His brother is after the killers. The fight occurred during a heavy rainstorm. Love died at Las Vegas at 3:30 a.m. Thursday, July 20............'' (Ibid. July 20, 1899)

"The clew to the identity of the robbers was first obtained near where the train was held up by gathering up a torn envelope and putting it together, finding it was postmarked Springer and received at Cimarron, and addressed by a harness maker to G. W. Franks, on sending him a couple of Winchester scabbards. There are over one hundred men in the mountains in pursuit of the desperadoes. The excitement runs high in the mountain over the tragic death of Ed Farr and of the wounding of Love and Smith . . . Officers from Colorado and a posse of sixteen with horses and arms from Huerfano county left the railroad at Maxwell City for the trail of the robbers Tuesday. General Agent Thacker of the Wells Fargo Company from San Francisco is on the ground conducting the pursuit of the train robbers who are yet in the mountains in the Ponil country. The pursuit is handicapped on account of continuous rains throughout the mountains and country. . . . . .

"U. S. Marshal Forsaker has about thirty pounds of dynamite, the tree of a pack saddle taken by the robbers from the express car at Folsom, and other stuff that was found in the cave in the mountains vacated by them. A hat and slicker were also found, indicating that the bandits had hurriedly vacated the place.

"One of the men is supposed to be Ketchum, alias Black Jack, who was in a robbery about a year ago at the same place. The other two go by the names of McGinnis and Franks. The latter about two weeks ago received a 30-40 Winchester and 1,000 rounds of ammunition. They are supposed to be heading toward La Belle or Taos, U. S. Marshal C. M. Forsaker says that the posse which engaged the bandits Sunday was led by Deputy Marshal Elliott, not Sheriff Farr nor Detective Reno. The accounts first sent to the press were founded on statements made by Reno, who, Foraker says, soon after the fighting began, deserted Elliott's posse, and leaving his horse and rifle behind hurried back to Cimarron (a town of two hundred people according to the papers). A posse of fifteen men under the leadership of Elliott left Cimarron Tuesday afternoon in pursuit of the bandits. A big fight is anticipated, as the bandits seem to be determined not to be taken alive. One of them particularly is a dead shot and it is likely they will sell their lives dearly. According to the report of the U. S. Marshall the fight Sunday came about as follows:

"The posse had started up a canyon and were ambushed by the robbers. Sheriff Farr was shot through the wrist while in the open. Smith was the next man to be downed, being shot through the calf of the leg. The shooting seems to have been entirely the work of one man, McGinnis, who after downing Smith turned his attention to Farr who was behind a tree three feet in diameter. McGinnis pumped a dozen shots into the tree, using a 30-40 Winchester. The bullet that killed Farr probably passed through the edge of the tree, entered Farr's body near the heart and came out near the groin. His body fell on Smith. Shortly after the firing began one of the desperadoes was seen to fall. He attempted to rise a couple of times, but failed, then moved no more . . . His body could not be found afterward. After killing Farr, McGinnis turned his attention to Deputy Sheriff Love. On exposing a leg to view, Love received a bullet near the thigh. After the shooting of Love, both parties suspended hostilities, and the posse, with the exception of Reno, stayed there during the night. During the fight two of the four horses belonging to the bandits were killed, one of the horses being a A-V horse belonging to W. G. Urton of Roswell. The trio are supposed to be McGinnis of Magdalena, G. W. Franks, and the notorious Ketchum, who is supposed to have operated with Black Jack's Gang . . . '' (Ibid—July 18, 1899).

One of the best known figures of the area was Mason Chase who had quite an apple orchid and was outstanding as a stockman. In 1924 he dictated many of his experiences. These papers lay in his attic even years after his death. Not only were they interesting reading but much of what is valued as history is found among them. Two items are outstanding: The Parson Tolby murder and the arrest of Sam Ketchum. His account fills in the gap of what took place from the time Reno brought in the news of the fight to the arrest of Sam Ketchum. It is seven handwritten pages; all one paragraph, phonetic spelling, and rapid fire words like talking rather than writing.

''Twenty-five years ago northern New Mexico had become civilized, and the population had become for the most part law-bidding; southern New Mexico and Arizona were still filled with desperadoes, train robbers and fighting murderous Indian tribes. About this time an old Texas ranger and frontier cowboy drifted into the little town of Cimarron. He had turned freighter. He has sixteen Spanish mules hooked to his three old fashioned freight wagons and driven with a jerk line. He had left Socorro county and drifted north. At this time there was quite a little activity in and near old Elizabethtown and Billy Morgan found work for himself and little mules hauling freight from Springer to Elizabethtown. Billie,

like many of the old type to which he belonged, saw everything, but said nothing. About a year later three strangers
dropped into Cimarron. They bought cartridiges, tobacco
and a small supply of grub and rode out of town. About a
week later they appeared again, loitered about town a
few hours, made about the same purchases as before and
rode away. This happened a number of times. Finally,
our leading merchant and post master (Hunt) began to
inquire about these men. Billie, who had just driven in
with his load of freight, started for the postoffice and
right at the door met the three strangers. He paid no attention, walked up and called for his mail, started out the
door when the postmaster called him back and took him
into his private office and said: "Mr. Morgan, I wonder
who those three men are that just went out?" "You
mean those three fellows I just met at the door?" 'Yes.'
'Why that's McGinnis, Sam Ketchum and Franks, three
of the toughest men in southern New Mexico and Arizona.' "What do you suppose they are doing here?" "I
don't suppose,' said Billie, 'I know. They are resting up,
getting the lay of the country and getting ready to hold
up some bank or train.' This information was quickly
sent to the sheriff's office. Banks were notified to be on
the lookout. The little stores and postoffices over the
country refused to carry any cash. One or two men, old
Billie among them, were deputised and requested to keep
an eye on these strangers. But they came and went, riding into the little town of Cimarron and out, as they saw
fit. They occasionally visited Elizabethtown. This went
on for more than three months; then one a.m. early in
August the country was thrown into excitement, the train
on the C. & S. R. R. at a point between the towns of
Folsom and Clayton had been held up and the mail and
express car robbed. Everyone in Cimarron jumped to
the same conclusion: The three robbers! They had done
this! The sheriff from Trinidad, Colorado, with the chief

detective of the C. & S. R. R. and other officers were rushed that night to the scene of the hold-up.

"At daybreak they took up the trail. It had been a dark rainy night. At first the trail was hard to follow as the downpour of rain had almost obliterated the horse tracks. By ten o'clock the officers had reached a point where the robbers had passed after the storm was over. The trail led directly west. The officers knew they were on the right track as the trail never followed a road nor went near any of the ranch houses scattered along the route. The officers followed the trail to where it crossed the Red River. Darkness came on and they had to wait for daylight. At the first streak of dawn they took up the trail; it led directly west to the foothills and into the Ponil canyon. The officers came into Cimarron to get more help and more information. Here old Billie joined them. The trail led up Draw canyon a short distance and up over the hill and down into Turkey canyon. The detective and officers from Colorado were jubilant and excited; they knew they were close upon the robbers. They did not know, or did not realize, the type of men they were following. They were riding up the dark trail that led up Turkey canyon, laughing and joking now that within a few hours they would be going back to Trinidad with the train robbers bound and driven ahead of them. Old Billie said to the leader: "You fellows need not think you are going to a Sunday school picnic. I know the birds we are following. Whenever you come on to them hell will tear loose.' 'Why,' said the officer, 'There are eleven of us and only three of them. Come on.'

"About this time one of the party discovered a little column of smoke arising. Bille and those from Cimarron knew that the outlaws were camped by the little spring a few hundred yards away, farther up the canyon. They suggested to the officer in charge that they scatter out and surround the robbers, to which the officer replied: 'Charge them!' He gave the spurs to his horse and charged out into the open, calling upon the robbers to surrender. This order was answered by a volley of shots from up the canyon. Hell had torn loose. Each officer sought shelter behind logs, rocks or trees. Darkness was coming on. Shots were being fired from every quarter. Ed Farr, the noble sheriff from Colorado, was standing behind a large pine tree. Just back of him a young tenderfoot was crouching. Suddenly Farr threw up his hands and fell back squarely on top of the little tenderfoot. One robber in particular was doing the effective shooting as he had the only vantage point and in old Billie's words— 'I knew this bird was going to get us all if somebody did not stop him. I crawled up to a rock, peaked over, spotted him and took aim as if he were an old buck and I were a starving to death. At the crack of my gun his music stopped and the firing almost ceased.'

"Darkness settled down about them. No man dared to move. There was nothing to do but wait for the light of day. The officers knew that the robbers had gone but if a man moved about some of his own friends might shoot him, thinking he was one of the bandits. So in this way each man waited not knowing what moment he might be shot. Finally day broke. The few officers who were still left in hiding about the little park began to peer about. Sheriff Farr was dead. The tenderfoot shot through the calf of the leg, another officer seriously wounded. He later died from the wound. The leader of the officers was lost, strayed or stolen. The bandits had vanished.

"The detective—leader of the officers—came into Cimarron the next a.m. with guns gone, coat gone and reported the robbers as all killed and the officers as either all killed or wounded. He had stayed until he had seen the last robber fall and then came to town for help. But old Billie said that this fellow had run down the canyon before he could tie up his mare. Some three days later one of the robbers sneaked into a ranch house near Ute Park and asked for help. The old man and his wife who lived at the ranch gave him food and bound up his wounds and tried to get him into the house, but he said, 'No. There had been some trouble and this might make you trouble. I guess I'll stay outside here at this shed.' The old man carried him out bedding and made the poor fugitive as comfortable as possible. Late that evening one of the old man's sons returned from Cimarron, went to the stable to put up his horse, saw the man lying in the make-shift bed, rushed to his father and asked: 'Who is that in the grainary?' The old man said: 'Oh, it's some man who has been wounded.' And the boy said that it was one of the train robbers and there was a thousand dollar reward for him. I am going into Cimarron to report this to the officers and to collect that reward.'

"He slipped out, caught his pony, and not daring to go near the shed to get his saddle, rode back to Cimarron where the detective leader and officer was still hanging about. He reported to him what he had seen. A posse of men, four in number, quickly gathered and under the same leadership, started for Ute Park. When they arrived there they called the old man out from his house and inquired the best way to approach the wounded robber without danger to themselves. "Why,' the old man said, "He can't harm you. He is scarcely able to move. He has no rifle. He has nothing but a six-shooter.' The detective said he had come up against such men before. It was arranged that one of the old man's small boys go into the grainary where the wounded man was and bring him a cup of coffee. When the robber raised up to take the coffee the boy was to pick up the pistol pretending to examine it. This was done. And Mr. Brave Detective! When he saw through the crack that the little boy had the pistol he rushed in and ordered the poor wounded man to get up and come with him. This poor Sam Ketchum was hardly able to do as his right shoulder had been almost shot away, the bone shattered and blood poison had set in. But the detective gave him a kick and said: 'Damm you.' The old ranchman, who was a veteran of the Civil War, poked Mr. Detective in the belly with an old muzzle loader and said: 'You stand back. This man is a wounded prisoner, and I know what he is doing if you don't.' Ketchum was brought to Cimarron and on to Springer in an open rig, then placed in the Santa Fe penitentiary for safe keeping, where he died a few days later from the effects of his wound. The boy who came to Cimarron to notify Mr. Detective is still waiting for his reward . . . ''

Wounded as he was, Sam could not forget that kick. When the spring wagon arrived at Cimarron and drew up at the St. James Hotel, Reno jumped down to tell everybody how he captured the outlaw. Ketchum leaped to his feet and reached for the Winchester left on the front seat. George Crocker saw the move and snatched the rifle before Sam could firmly grasp it. He was not as anxious to break away as he was to take care of the man who kicked him when he was down. He joked with Henry Lambert as he prepared a room for him in the hotel. Later a sheepherder told of seeing a man lying naked by a small spring. He had tied his saddle blanket by its four corners to four bushes and kept pouring water atop the blanket. The water seeped through to wash the wound in his side and to cool off the fever. It evidently worked for McGinnis eventually recovered to be captured far from the Turkey canyon hideout. He had used an old Indian method for the cure which would rather be called miraculous since a saddle blanket would hardly drip clean water into a wound, especially a blanket as loaded with dirt and grime as his was. Meantime where ever Tom Ketchum worked he was mapping out in his own mind another bold attempt on the Colorado and Southern believing it to be the second. The story of his life would hereby have changed had he any inkling that the second claimed the life of his brother. What reasons he had for going it alone he took to the grave.

"Samuel Ketchum, accused of train robbery, murder and resisting U. S. officers, was brought to the Santa Fe penitentiary last evening from Springer by U. S. Marshal C. M. Forsaker of Albuquerque, J. N. Thacker, secret service agent of the Wells Fargo Express Company and W. F. Powers of Albuquerque, route agent of the express company.

"Ketchum was very weak last evening from the loss of blood and the pain of his wound in the left arm. This forenoon he rested easily, although he said his arm seemed to weigh about three hundred pounds. Forsaker Thacker and Powers were at the penitentiary nearly all day and toward noon were joined by Governor Otero, Chief Justice Mills, Judge McFie and District Clerk A. M. Bergere. These discussed the case thoroughly, and the result of the conference was that every effort will be exerted in bringing in the other two of the Gang that robbed the train near Folsom.

"The officers are very reluctant to speak about the capture of Ketchum. In fact they think too much has been published already and that considerable sent out from Cimarron, Springer and Las Vegas is untrue. The Marshall had asked Detective Reno not to wire the story until all of the facts had been ascertained, but it seems that the news was told at once anyway. The posse that came upon the robbers was commanded by Elliott, but Forsaker had placed discretionary power in Sheriff Farr. The story of the fight is told in yesterday's dispatches and is virtually correct except perhaps the statement about special officer Reno who is accused of cowardice, against whom there is bitter feeling at Cimarron. The officers who brought Ketchum to the penitentiary would express no opinion for publication on the merits of the case, but in private expressed themselves forcibly and freely.

"The case is entirely in the hands of U. S. Marshall Foraker, who, with the assistance of the Wells Fargo people, has a posse of ten men pursuing the robbers, who are fleeing toward the northwest. The story that hundreds of men are in pursuit, including a posse from Colorado, is declared absurd. Ketchum may be tried by the Territory. He waived a preliminary hearing before U. S. Commissioner Seabury at Springer, and his bail on the charge of robbery was fixed at $10,000, while on the charge of murder he could not be bailed.

"Ketchum is six feet tall, has a sandy mustache and complexion, blue eyes and freckled face and hands. He came to New Mexico from San Angelo, Texas, and, according to Marshall Foraker, is the most desperate character in the Territory. He is the brother of Tom Ketchum, one of the many reputed 'Black Jacks' implicated in the train robbery at Folsom two years ago. Tom is thirty-seven years of age while Sam is about Forty-five. No criminal charge has been brought against Sam Ketchum although he has enjoyed the notoriety of being a desperate character. He will not speak for publication, but has spoken freely to the officers. According to his story, after the fight, while it was still daylight, his two companions assisted him on a horse several times but he was so weak that he became faint everytime and had to dismount. Finally, he said, 'Go on, boys, and leave me.' Two of his companions rode away then, and Ketchum made his way to a near by farm house asking for assistance. Officers were notified and arrested Ketchum without his offering any resistance. Marshall Foraker does not think it possible that the robbers left their camp in daylight, although Ketchum's story is borne out by one of the posse, who said he saw the robbers riding away.

"It is now denied that two of the horses of the robbers were killed although that was the story given out first. The robbers had no bedding at the camp, and left behind them everything including thirty pounds of giant powder, coffee, bacon and flour. They procured nothing of value from the train but took a saddle tree. A brother of Sheriff Farr came to Springer to take charge of the body. Sheriff

Farr was killed by a bullet that had passed through two inches of wood of the tree behind which Farr was standing, pierced his heart and passed out at the groin. It is the fact of Reno's leaving Farr's body that has caused such feeling against him. It is said that he ran as fast as his legs could carry him after saying to Smith, who was wounded and lying by Farr's body, that he would go and bring assistance. Reno left his gun and other belongings behind and never said anything to the other members of the posse who were in shelter seventy-five yards away. When Reno first entered Cimarron he reported that every one of the posse had been shot. It was not twelve o'clock when he came in as first reported but seven o'clock in the morning. It is reported that Marshall Foraker asked Reno to go back with him to find the bodies of the dead men but Reno refused to go back with him saying that he had to go to Springer to wire some messages.

"Marshall Foraker says that he does not know who the other two bandits are and the supposition that they are men named McGinnis and Franks is mere guess work. It is difficult at this time to get at the truth of the various statements published. None of the officials who brought Ketchum to the penitentiary are willing to make any official statement as none of them are eyewitnesses of the fight or that part of the chase which resulted in the capture of Ketchum. The trial will, however, bring out the facts of the case and will settle the dispute that has arisen between officer Reno and others. If tried on a charge against the United States (mail robbery) Ketchum will be tried at Las Vegas. If the Territorial charge against him (train robbery) is given the first chance the trial will take place at Raton.

"Officer Reno whom U. S. Marshall Foraker intimated deserted his comrades in the fight with the train robbers near Cimarron, says of the battle: 'We reached the robbers camp about five p.m. We were then in single file, following a narrow trail. Wilson Elliott of Trinidad,

65

with four men, went to the right of the camp, while Mr. Farr, Smith and myself went to the left side to better cover the ground. The firing began immediately. My position was to the right of Farr, about five feet. I crossed over and took a position nearer the robbers camp about ten feet from Farr and Smith who were behind one tree. Shortly after the shooting began Smith fell and Farr was shot in the right hand. He wrapped his hand up and asked me if I could locate the robber who was firing at us from across the canyon.

"Almost immediately I heard a groan and saw Farr fall back on Smith. He gradually sank down and Smith told me he was dead. The firing continued until six p.m. when all was quiet. I remained at my post two hours after the firing ceased, watching the robbers horses; thinking the robbers might come for them. A gray horse was about seventy-five yards distant. When too dark to see the sights on my gun, I went over to Farr and Smith who were stretched out at the next tree, only ten feet distant. I felt Farr's forehead which was cold, and removed him from E. H. Smith who was suffering intensely from a gunshot wound through the left leg. I asked him if he could go with me and he replied, 'No.' He asked me to get help at once. I left my rifle with him and started for Cimarron afoot, over the mountains, as it is almost an impassable place in daylight with a horse. I got lost about midnight, and remained on the mountain, wet through, until day began to break, when I found my way into Cimarron, about seven a.m. and notified U. S. Marshall Foraker of the fight with the robbers, informing him I had not seen anything of Elliott and his men after the battle began, but heard their rifles until about six p.m. when the two last shots were fired by the robbers, and I was apprehensive for Mr. Elliott and his men .... " *SANTA FE NEW MEXICAN* July 22, 1899)

The news on the following day dealt mostly with the arrest of one David Carver, at Springer, because he was believed implicated in the robbery near Folsom. This no doubt was Will Carver whose very speech showed him up as a Texan and added to the circumstantial evidence since McGinnis, Sam Ketchum and the others of the Black Jack Gang were said to be from Texas. It looked bad for Carver who had to do a lot of explaining as to why he was in Springer at this particular time. He offered what seemed a satisfactory answer and was released. With McGinnis wounded and Sam Ketchum on his way to the McBride ranch Carver decided that the best place to hide out was in the open. Nobody in the posse actually knew what he looked like; the explanation for the letter seemed to satisfy the officials. He seems to have been ill with the small-pox. Once they let him go he was a hard man to find again. He was next seen far away from Springer. The posse and officials in Springer were too keen on picking up Franks and McGinnis to hold a man evidently sick at the time of the robbery. The paper also stated that James B. McBride put in official claim for the five hundred dollar reward offered for the arrest of Sam Ketchum. Since he had summoned the officers he felt that he had entire claim to the money. It was not the amount he expected but he was satisfied and had no intentions of dividing it among the posse. The readers were also advised that Jefferson B. Farr was made sheriff to fill the vacancy left by the sudden death of his brother.

"Awards amounting to $1,400 are offered for the capture, dead or alive, of Wm H. McGinnis and G. W. Franks, the two men alleged to have assisted in the robbery of the Colorado & Southern train near Folsom. Brothers of Sheriff Farr of Colorado, who was killed by the robbers, offer $400 of this amount, and the rest is offered by the Wells Fargo Express Company and the Colorado & Southern Railroad. The men are supposed to be with Tom Ketchum in Texas. Ketchum lived in Tom Green county and has many influential friends among the stockmen of Western Texas. The sheriff and his posse are well armed and prepared for a desperate resistance. Tom Ketchum has a reputation among Texas authorities of being the most depserate outlaw in the Southwest. It is said he led the band that held up and robbed a through California passenger train on the Southern Pacific road near Lozier, Texas, three years ago (1896), securing from the Wells Fargo safe more than $40,000 cash. They were pursued over more than 400 miles through West Texas by Rangers and U. S. Marshalls, but escaped to New Mexico. It is claimed that shortly afterward Tom Ketchum and his brother Sam Ketchum, who was fatally wounded in the battle with train officers near Folsom, New Mexico, recently, participated in the Texas & Pacific train robbery near Coleman, Texas, securing the express company's safe. It is supposed they fled to Arizona and committed other train robberies, but were pressed hard by officers, and sought refuge in New Mexico where they remained until a short time ago, when they re-entered Texas and planned the last train robbery in New Mexico. Tom Ketchum was raised a few miles north of Austin. He is a little over thirty years of age, and before entering on his career of crime was widely known in that section as a dead shot with rifle and pistol.'' (*SANTA FE NEW MEXICAN*, August 1, 1899.)

The Lozier, Coleman and Stanton hold-ups seemed to be of little concern to the Texas Rangers. Webb, in his book THE TEXAS RANGERS makes no reference at all to the four-hundred-mile chase. The year the Ketchums seem to have gotten away with so much money was dedicated to preventing a prize fight between Bob Fitzsimmons and Pete Maher at El Paso. Practically the entire Ranger force was sent to the border town to prevent the fight. A forty thousand dollar hold-up is of little consequence against what gamblers were pouring into the Fitzsimmons-Maher fight on both sides of the border. Naturally, the Rangers couldn't be everywhere at once which is what Kid Lewis knew when he held up the City

National Bank at Wichita Falls, getting only six hundred dollars for his trouble, having killed the cashier and wounded the book-keeper during the hold-up. Horse thieves operating in the Glass Mountains also kept Rangers busy so as to make the Lozier attempt comparatively easy. At the penitentiary Sam Ketchum was given Number 129. Every plea to have him undergo surgery for the shattered arm was denied. Despite the blood poisoning he insisted that he would rather go to the grave with two arms than one. Tom was to have very much the same trouble but consented to amputation. He recovered to march to the gallows. Sam died July 24, 1899.

CHAPTER THREE

Otero throws out the window the Indian blanket-water
cure for McGinnis by having Franks bring him to the
adobe home of a native family friendly to the bandits.
These agreed to nurse McGinnis back to health for which
Franks amply rewarded them by alleviating their finan-
cial stress. Franks continued on heading for Roswell and
Carlsbad country where a rancher named Lusk had been
caring for some horses for the Black Jack Gang. He
would wait for McGinnis at this ranch.

"McGinnis remained with this family for about four
weeks and received the best attention possible. Either
the man or his wife was with him day and night and his
wounds were kept clean and dressed every day. So far as
McGinnis knew, no one suspected his being there. By the
middle of August he had entirely recovered, so he decided
to leave for the Lusk ranch. His Mexican friends cried on
the day of McGinnis departure, for they had tended him
like one of the family. The robber showed the greatest
appreciation and affection for both man and wife and
presented each with a goodly sum of money with his
thanks and a promise to come back and see them at some
future day. His horse was in fine condition, and he left
his benefactors at night, well equipped with rifle, pistols,
and sufficient food to last until he reached his rendezvous
with Franks.

"Soon after the arrival of McGinnis at the ranch,
Lusk became suspicious and notified M. Cicero Stewart,
Sheriff of Eddy county, of the two suspicious strangers
at his place. Accordingly, on August 22, 1899, Sheriff

71

Stewart, together with two deputies, J. C. Cantrell and Rufus Thomas, went with Lusk to arrest the men. When they arrived, McGinnis was in the house, eating breakfast, while Franks was outside hunting their horses. A slight noise made by the posse while tying their horses to a wire fence alarmed McGinnis, who rushed out of the door to get his rifle from his saddle. Seeing Thomas approaching the house, he fired at the latter with his 45 Colt revolver, striking him in the shoulder. Observing the ranchman, Lusk, in the group, and being satisfied that he had turned informer, he aimed at him, wounding him in the wrist. By this time Lusk had gotten his rifle into action and fired a shot which struck the outlaw on the side of the head. As McGinnis was stunned, he was quickly disarmed, handcuffed, and tied on a horse. Meanwhile, Franks, who had watched these proceedings from a hill about a mile away, disappeared. He was never captured, but his partner was taken safely back to town. The Colfax county officials having been notified of the arrest, the sheriff and two deputies went to Carlsbad and escorted McGinnis to Raton . . . ' (Otero o.c. pp 117-18)

"Sheriff Stewart of Eddy county and posse captured at daylight near Carlsbad, a man supposed to be one of the Ketchum Gang in the Folsom robbery. He made a fight and shot two of the posse, one dangerously. He also shows several bullet wounds just healing. His partner escaped. The captured one gives the name Tom Johnson. He gave a desperate battle even when disarmed and overpowered. It was necessary to stun and tie him. Sheriff Stewart deserves great credit for his capture, as there was an exciting fight." (*SANTA FE NEW MEXICAN* quoting a dispatch from Carlsbad August 16, 1899)

"U. S. Marshall Foraker leaves in the morning for Santa Fe with train robber McGinnis. McGinnis has been positively identified by J. K. Hunt, a merchant of Cimarron. Special Agent Reno and Sheriff Farr, brother of the murdered sheriff, are here. Franks has escaped. Sheriff

Stewart was unable to trail him. The latter officer, however, has made an excellent record by the capture of McGinnis and easily ranks as the leader of all Eddy county sheriffs. This man and one other called at the Lusk ranch, twenty miles from Carlsbad, to secure horses left on the range several months ago, which had been stolen in Arizona. While the couple were there, by previous arrangements with a ranchman, a courier was sent to notify Sheriff Stewart that the claimants for the horses had come. The sheriff, accompanied by J. D. Cantrell and Ruffus Thomas, by a night ride reached the place, and at daylight saw one of the outlaws enter a tent for breakfast. The other man remained at a dry camp half a mile distant. The hidden posse got tired of waiting for him to come to the ranch tent and started to capture the one at breakfast. They ran up against a wire fence, however, and made so much noise that the outlaw was alarmed and made a dash to his horse having left his rifle on the saddle. The hunted man shot deputy Thomas in the shoulder with a revolver, and wounded ranchman Lusk, who had betrayed them, slightly in the wrist. Sheriff Stewart fired a shot that grazed the skull of the combatant and stunned him so that he was captured and disarmed. He, however, struck the sheriff and sought to grab a revolver from one of the posse. The other one of the fugitives watched the fight from afar and rode away in haste. A posse is trailing him. The pony ridden by the captured outlaw is branded BD connected. The brand is given by Andy Jones of Sterling, Texas. The saddle is marked S.H.M. on the seat, and is supposed to be owned by Sam Murry of Ozona, Texas. The arms used by the outlaws are a 30-40 U. S. Army Winchester and a .45 caliber Colt revolver. The Winchester scabbard is marked in plain gothic letters "To Youmma" the m inverted and indistinct. The Winchester is a new gun, and this fact also connects the prisoner in a manner with the Folsom robbery, as a gun of this description was used by this Gang, having been

73

shipped from Denver to the Folsom outlaws." (*SANTA FE NEW MEXICAN* quoting dispatch from Carlsbad August 22, 1899)

"Trial of McGinnis — A telegraphed report from Raton says: The witnesses examined in the McGinnis case Thursday (October 5) gave evidence tending to prove that the defendant was a member of the Black Jack Gang which held up the Colorado & Southern express train at Folsom, July 11. The defendant strongly objected to this evidence being introduced contending that McGinnis was on trial for the murder of Sheriff Farr and not for holding up the train. Judge Mills, however, overruled the objection, and the case was proceeded with. The evidence on the train robbery connecting McGinnis therewith seems to be complete. The defense, however, is not cross questioning the witnesses who testify regarding the train robbery, maintaining its position that the two crimes cannot be connected. It is reserving the principal fight for the murder case, the hearing of witnesses on which will be commenced in the morning.

"The testimony so far given tends to show that it was Black Jack's Gang that held up the train July 11, and that Wm. H. McGinnis was one of the members of that Gang. There were Thursday twelve more witnesses to be examined in behalf of the prosecution before the defense will be opened. The defense intends to show that the posse under Marshall Foraker, which was attempting to arrest the bandits at the time Sheriff Farr was killed, was not a posse within the meaning of the law, and had no proper authority to act as such. The courtroom was inadequate for the people who tried to obtain admittance and many were turned away. An evening session of the court was held lasting until eleven o'clock . . . " (S.F.N.M. Oct. 7, 1899)

"At Raton, Saturday evening, the jury, after deliberating three hours, found a verdict of guilty in the case of William H. McGinnis, charged with the murder of Sheriff

Edward Farr of Walsenburg, Colorado. The testimony of James H. Morgan, one of the posse, was favorable to the defendant. Other members of the posse had testified that at the time of the attempt to arrest the robbers in Turkey Canyon the defendant McGinnis had a rifle in his hand, and immediately upon being ordered to surrender raised his rifle to his shoulder and fired in the direction of Farr, and that Farr fired simultaneously. Morgan's testimony conflicted with this. He said that at the moment the shots were fired McGinnis had no gun or rifle, and that he fell immediately upon the first fire of the posse.

"Miguel Lopez testified that Perfecto Cordova had told him after the fight with the robbers that McGinnis had no rifle when first seen by the posse. Cordova swore on the stand that McGinnis had a rifle in his hand when first discovered. The defendant then took the stand and said he was in Turkey canyon July 16, 1899, in company with two other people, but refused to name them: That he was getting supper about 5:30 in the evening and had started to a small creek about fifty yards from their camp to get some water, carrying a canteen in his hand; that when he got about half way to the creek he heard the report of a gun and he felt a pain in his shoulder, as if some one had struck him a heavy blow with a club; that immediately another shot was fired from the direction of Farr, which struck him in the back and brought him to the ground; that he tried to move but could not; that he had laid on the ground several minutes unable to move; that all the time there was a perfect volley of shots fired in the direction of the camp; that he fainted away and knew nothing more of what took place until about dusk, when he regained consciousness and found one of his companions standing over him, asking him how badly he was hurt.

"The man he afterward admitted to be Franks. He stated that he and Franks then went to where Sam Ketchum had fallen in the rocks, some distance away and there they found Ketchum so badly wounded that he was unable to mount his horse. After some conversation with Ketchum, Franks and McGinnis decided to leave Ketchum and seek safety in flight. On cross examination defendant refused to answer many questions asked by the prosecution. All questions relating to his former life, his acquaintance with the Black Jack Gang, he refused absolutely to reply to, and would only answer relating to the fight in which Farr was killed. When questioned about the train robbery at Folsom he refused to answer. When counsel for the Territory attempted to compel him to answer these questions, McGinnis addressed the court saying: 'If it please the court, I am here on trial for murder. I understand there are other charges against me for train robbery and murder. I have been put on trial without any chance of procuring many of my witnesses. I have no other way to protect myself. And I positively refuse to answer any question except those asked me concerning this fight, and I will not under any circumstances answer any other questions'' (S.F.N.M. Oct. 9, 1899)

The most neglected figure throughout was H. N. Love. Sheriff Edward Farr holds the spotlight and Love is brought in as an after thought. Yet he did give his life in pursuit of train robbers. Instead of a separate murder trial for each, the trial was for the murder of Farr and Love but Leahy and Bunker managed to keep the questioning centered around the killing of Farr. Leahy also sought to bring in the train robbery at Folsom. Turning to Judge Mills McGinnis said: "If the court please, I am here on trial for murder. I understand there are other charges against me for train robbery, other murder charges, and for interfering with the United States mail. I have no way of protecting myself against these charges since they do not pertain to the case in hand. I positively refuse to answer any further questions except those pertaining to the fight at Turkey canyon. I will not, under any circumstances whatsoever answer any other questions that tend to incriminate me.''

"McGinnis proved an exceptionally good witness, both as to intelligence and courage. His answers were prompt, without the slightest hesitation or show of fear and I believe that he told the absolute truth. It was very unfortunate for him that the trial took place just about a month after the conviction of Black Jack at Clayton. Public opinion was aroused to a high pitch against all persons connected with train robberies, and the courts were determined to stop this crime which gave New Mexico such a bad name for lawlessness, even though all points of law were not adhered to literally. Personally, I believe that all courts should be impartial and just at all times. Sometimes, however, popular clamor and political ambitions combine to banish the calm and careful consideration due to justice.

"Being greatly interested in the case, I went to Raton and on the invitation of Chief Justice Mills sat beside him during the proceedings. I listened very attentively to all the witnesses. I do not pretend to know what changed Perfecto Cordova, but any person who heard his testimony could tell that he was following instructions. In fact after the trial, he admitted to several that he had been mistaken about McGinnis firing his gun. I was particularly impressed with Morgan's testimony and believed that he and McGinnis had told the truth. I noticed that every ruling in the case was against the defendant. I have never believed that McGinnis had a fair trial; it seemed to me that he was convicted before he was tried. From all of the evidence given at the trial, I came to the conclusion that Franks killed both Sheriff Farr and H. N. Love, as both McGinnis and Ketchum were down and out after the first volley of bullets fired by the posse.

"When the arguments had all been finished, the jury deliberated for three hours, finally bringing in a verdict of guilty of murder in the second degree. The court thus sentenced McGinnis to the penitentiary for life. Perhaps it was fortunate for him that he was not tried for train robbery, because he might have received the same sentence given Black Jack ... McGinnis proved a model prisoner, never violating a rule of the penitentiary, He was a trusty for some time and on two occasions assisted the authorities in suppressing outbreaks by the convicts.

"The first mutiny occurred at four o'clock in the morning, when two prisoners, who were being conducted from the cell house to the bakery, attacked the deputy warden and locked him up in the key room. They were equipped with pistols and ammunition, which had been smuggled in by a discharged convict, and could help themselves to any keys they wanted. They tried to capture the armory but met determined resistance from the prison guards who knew that, if they succeeded, it would mean many deaths and very serious trouble. A large number of shots were exchanged in the fight and the night captain of the guards was seriously wounded, as well as a trusty, Pedro Sandoval. The mutiny was finally suppressed and the two convicts were shot. One died during the night and the other died a few days later in the penitentiary hospital. The captain of the guard and the trusty recovered. During this affair McGinnis was night engineer at the power plant. He remained loyal to the authorities and helped suppress the mutiny. Without his timely assistance many others would have been killed. The other insurrection occurred some years later. On this occasion they used a young boy, the brother-in-law of Superintendent Bursum, as a shield to keep the guards from firing on them. Armed with knives, the prisoners surrounded the cell house keepers and demanded the keys to the armory. Mrs. Bursum; Mrs. James, wife of the deputy warden; and Mrs. Martin, wife of the penitentiary clerk; ran to the top story of the administration building, where they could see the mutinous convicts below. They called out to McGinnis, who was a trusty, to get help. Jumping on a gray racer belonging to Mr. Martin, the latter rode a mile to town. In a short time he returned with a squad of Territorial militia and the mutiny was soon over. Accordingly, on the eve of the next regular holiday, July 1, 1905, upon recommendation of penitentiary authorities, I issued an order commuting McGinnis' sentence to a term of ten years. As a matter of fact, McGinnis was released on January 10, 1906, as his actual time was shortened by good behavior to six years and three months. After he became free, McGinnis, whose real name was W. E. Lay, was in the saloon business at Shoshoni (northeast of Riverton on present Highway 20, (pop. 827) Wyoming, for a short time. Later he became interested in oil lands and moved to Los Angeles. He married a very fine woman and they had two children. Mrs. Lay told a friend that I was the only person about whom her husband spoke in the very highest terms." (Otero, o.c. pp 129-131)

Franks escaped to South America returning several years after the death of Black Jack. He rode into Cimarron and gave his name as Pegleg Sullivan. He was both liberal and jovial which contributed much to his popularity. Unable to shake off the flu and realizing his end was near he told Fred Lambert that he was the Franks long sought in the Turkey Canyon fight. He had dug up the money buried by the Gang, which was the reason for his liberality. Having spent most of the money during those months in Cimarron there was enough left to defray the expense of his funeral. The little that was remained, and it was hardly worth mailing, was sent to a niece. She was the only living relative Franks had left in the world.

Having skipped the Springer area, Carver went on to the WS Ranch near Alma where he was known to Captain French as a good worker. Fearful that the law might find him he soon left Alma and returned to San Angelo, Texas. Carver had known Butch Cassidy for quite some time. Indeed Cassidy was better acquainted with Carver than he was with either of the Ketchums. Carver was with

Max Stein, Tom Capehart, Frank Laughton when they made an attempt on Tombstone but had to leave one jump ahead of the posse. For the next few weeks outlaws and posse play hide and seek around Rustlers Park at Sam Simon valley in Arizona. George A. Scarborough, employed by the Cattle Growers Association to track down rustlers knew many of the hideouts of the Black Jack Gang having been with the posses that hunted the outlaws during the years 1898 and 1899. With several followers he ferreted out rustlers in the Burrow Mountains and the Alkali country just northwest of Lordsburg. A fresh trail led into the San Simon country. Here they came upon the carcass of a freshly killed beef and followed all the telltale signs which brought them directly to the camp of the rustlers. In the battle that followed Carver stood his ground firing away at Scarborough and his men. Birchfield seeing that Scarborough was wounded in the leg pulled him to a place of safety and did what he could to stop the flow of blood. The rustlers managed to escape. Realizing there was little he could do for Scarborough, Birchfield decided to go for help, despite the handicap of his own wound. Placed on a wagon after a night of torture in the sleet and rain, he was put on a train at Stein's Pass and rushed to the hospital at Deming, but died several days later. Carver, morose and surly through the years because of a faithless wife, fired the shot but expose and loss of blood did the rest. Scarborough was one of the great lawmen of the Southwest in favor of some who were actually lesser lights in courage.

While Carver was square-jawed and square shouldered Harvey Logan, his friend and associate was thin faced, sported a mustache and walked with a slight droop of the shoulder. In the photo of the Wild Bunch that is shown in every book dealing with outlaws of the Southwest these are the two that are standing. Carver has the look of a dude; Logan a look of defiance even to the rakish way his hat sits back on his head. Carver has his left hand on the shoulder of Harry Longabaugh seated in front of him, and his right hand on the shoulder of Ben Kilpatrick. His clothes show expensive taste and a love of the best that hold-up money can buy. The death of Scarborough scared Carver and the others into leaving the San Simon and western New Mexico country for the sparser regions of Nevada, Wyoming and Utah. They made more frequent visits to the hideout between Hanksville and Green River.

Tipton, between Table Rock and Red Desert, east of Bridger's Pass in Wyoming, was a small village on the Union Pacific line. The population in 1879 was given as twenty-five, and, while today it is on Highway 30 and the population is higher it is still a comparatively small town. Here, on the night of August 29, 1900, Cassidy, Logan, Longabaugh and Carver used the Black Jack method of holding up the train. Using three sticks of dynamite they blew open the safe in the express car and made off with several thousand dollars. Angered, the officials of the railroad offered a thousand dollars for each of the four the railroad detectives would capture. Even this tempting offer failed to meet with success on the part of the lawmen but served to stimulate the Gang into trying where the real money was—banks. Off to a hideout they went to enjoy talk, cards and target practice. Probably spent some of the money at Hanksville and some in Green River City, Wyoming, not to be confused with the Green River country in Utah. Whether it was because they were broke again, or for the thrill of a bank robbery, the next hold-up was the First National Bank at Winnemucca, present population 2,847 but then about 1500. It is nicely located on the Humboldt river in north central Nevada just east of Winnemucca Peak. The same four that held up the Number Three Passenger at Tipson participated in the bank robbery. Ben Kilpatrick seems to have been in on this robbery also, possibly as a "watch" since only four entered the bank. He may have had the care of the horses an important chore. Without horses they were lost, and they knew it. A gun shot, any noise would serve to stampede them; horses were somebody's responsibility in a hold-up.

After Winnemucca, with over thirty-two thousand dollars to spend, they traveled south to enjoy the Wheat Building Roof Garden and other delights in the city that was big time mingled with the range. Fort Worth will always be the cowboys town no matter how it grows. This was the place for the boys with its roof garden that sported a soda fountain, where seated couples were served lemonades and sarsaparilla, where one could order a refreshing drink of moxie and watch the play of lights on fancy selzer bottles. This was the town for Irish stew, German food and beer, Havana cigars, imposing carriages, tasseled Percherons strutting in front of beer wagons, all kinds of traffic and hard liquor. Of wine, women, and song, there was no end so long as the money lasted for these were not saving men—neither spiritually nor materially. Tomorrow there would be another bank somewhere between El Paso and the Canadian border. A tangle of electric wires ran in all directions in the business section. With a clang and a bang noisy trolleys swayed along raised tracks to the amusement of cowboys loitering on all corners and around recreation halls. The famous White Elephant Saloon was there when the boys hit town in November of 1900. Who can forget the White Elephant where Luke Short and Longhair Jim Courtright and so many of the frontier breed whiled away their time and lost their money, if not their lives. Winfield Scott, a stockman of means, thought well of the old White Elephant, well enough to buy it and to build an imposing structure to house it so that other stockmen of means could hoist a foot to the brass rail now that the day of the gunslinger was about over. There was still a little danger from the gamblers and toughs who frequented the neighboring saloons and, often resentful of the better class at the White Elephant, sought to "start something" in the hopes of having a good old time killing to keep the ball rolling as it were. Here one could see betimes McGraw of the New York Giants ball club, J. J. Corbett, J. L. Sullivan, Tex Rickard, Bat Masterson; so many turn of the century notables. Here neatly dressed, pockets buldging, the Wild Bunch, the Hole in the Wall Gang, the last of the Black Jack Gang sampled wines, munched foods, watched beautiful women, dreamed their tomorrows, black out their yesterdays, swayed with the muses, laughed with the great and near great, always paying in gold coin as becomes the idle rich. This was the life here at 606 Main Street, Forth Worth, Texas.

Up the next block John Swartz, on 705 Main, maintained a photographer's gallery. New derbys, new suits, new watch fobs, new shoes, new watch chains, new look, spic and span, two standing Longabaugh, Kilpatrick and Cassidy sitting in the midst of a backdrop of curtains, tassels and flowers, they posed like professionals. The three men in the front are not sitting on one long couch but on individual chairs as a study of the photo will reveal. Longabaugh is the only one who forgot to wipe the dust off his shoes. In 1900 even Fort Worth did not boast too many paved streets. After this they bought bicycles, which seemed to be the rage, rode up and down Main street, returned to their rooming house and slikered up again to escort some of the opposite sex readily recognized by make-up and manner as of easy virtue, to the joints. Women didn't drink or smoke in respectable places in those days, even in Fort Worth. Dance halls, brothals, gambling dens. These were different. But they spent more money in these places than the White Elephant. The women could tell them why. All the gold diggers were not in mining camps. Some of the world's most successful gold diggers never saw a mining town. Our interest in these men never lags simply because of their connection at one time or other with Black Jack Ketchum. Of the group

Kilpatrick and Carver were definitely members of Ketchum's crew of outlaws. The others participated in some of the hold-ups either in Mexico, Arizona, Utah or New Mexico but not as definite members. With Sam dead, Franks in South America, McGinnis in prison, Tom ready for the scaffold, this band grouped together mostly for safety in numbers. A lone detective would hardly play the hero in attempting to take the whole band if he held two six-shooters. They might have enjoyed Fort Worth for many more months had it not been for that really well taken photo. The Montpelier, Idaho, bank robbery is laid at the door of this Wild Bunch, as were a number of others. The Pinkerton Detective Agency sent its men swarming everywhere. The Wild Bunch had to stick together for many of these detectives posed as outlaws. Others were discovered to be cowboys, geologists, prospectors, gamblers, dudes, saddle-makers, blacksmiths. There was no trusting anybody anymore. The fellow working on a ranch with you might turn out to be a detective. The best thing to do was to hole up somewhere, strike miles from the hide-out, spend the money hundreds of miles away from the hold-up. This is the band that struck at Wagner, Montana, when the Great Northern train came to a halt, took in over a hundred thousand dollars in unsigned currency that had been intended for the Helena bank. A sheriff happened to be on the train. He opened fire but the exchange was too much for him. The men rode off. They scattered Indian fashion to confuse the posse. Their trails led off in so many directions the posse returned a very bitter but empty handed group. Banks and storekeepers were cautioned to watch for certain bills and asked to co-operate with the authorities in reporting tens or twenties that seemed freshly cut as often these were signed in an imaginary bank official's name for the purpose of trapping the outlaws. At least it would tell their whereabouts. No doubt this is what brought a detective to Fort Worth. It was Fred J. Dodge, the Wells

Fargo detective, who spotted Carver's picture in the window display at the photo shop. The others he didn't know, but Carver he knew because of the Black Jack Gang, the robberies at Stein's Pass, Twin Mountain and the border towns. He asked Swartz about the men and located the rooming house. They had checked out. They found out through the grape-vine that Dodge had been asking around. Where did they go? Who knows? To the moon perhaps. They paid their rent on time. That was all the land lady was interested in. That was her business. What they did was their own business. They checked out. She had no further interest in the former boarders. With a shrug of the shoulders Dodge left to try elsewhere. Somewhere somebody in Fort Worth knew where they went. Was it some cyprian who gave up the secret? Was it ingenuity on the part of the detective, or a combination of both? The end was in view but not because of Detective Dodge.

The outlaws stayed for a time in San Antonio following very much the routine of Fort Worth. They checked in at the best hotels, enjoyed the most expensive liquors, idled away time impressing the demireps who patiently listened and smiled and laughed so long as coins filled their empty hands. Cassidy and Longabaugh tired of this and thought to return to Wyoming or the hide out in Utah; Carver, Logan and Kilpatrick agreed that they were living more like libertines than gentlemen; in their own way they had an appreciation of the finer things in life but knew that as hunted men they could never really openly enjoy them. Carver, Kilpatrick and Logan went to Concho county in Texas, to the hill country near Eden where they hunted, slept, vacationed. Eden, the terminus of the Gulf, Colorado and Santa Fe railroad was where Kilpatrick went to school, grew up and learned to be a cowboy. Eden was too good to last. Logan (known to the Wild Bunch as Kid Curry) and Ben Kilpatrick (often referred to as The Tall Texan) spent much of the time together at a spring on the Mollay Cattle Company range. Cowboys noticed their fine horses and made talk, so much so that Dodson decided to go to the camp to look over the horses, more especially the brands, as he wanted no horse thieves on the range. All seemed in order. Several days later Oliver Thornton, once employed by Ed Dozier former sheriff of Concho county, came over to discuss the "keep your hogs out of my yard" problem. Good fences make good neighbors. There were lots of Kilpatricks about. The hogs belonged to Boone Kilpatrick but Thornton blamed Ed Kilpatrick and probably said some harsh things or at least loud enough to be heard by the Tall Texan, Carver and Logan who were enjoying a game of croquet. They came over and asked Thornton to leave as they were looking for no trouble. Ed said that Thornton came over armed with a musket; others claimed that he faced the group unarmed. Logan drew his six-shooter. Who knows why? Perhaps to scare the man off. As it turned out Thornton ran when he saw the action which prompted Logan to fire several shots. Thornton fell over a log and into the spring, where his wife later found him. It was found that he had a wound in the forehead and two in the body. Ed Kilpatrick rode to Eden to report to the authorities that there was a dead man at the spring. Mostly to protect Ed the others hit for the hills. The posse soon became aware that it was not dealing with amateurs. They found the telephone line cut at the Mollay station, as well as the wires to the little town of Eldorado in Schleicher county. Gray & Murchison located a store here in 1895 and gave the community the name Eldorado. A school was built in 1897 and at the time the Gang was vacationing at the spring it was made the county seat. Today its population is a little over a thousand. Here Carver, Kilpatrick and Logan posed as pony buyers but found nothing to their taste. They did buy two horses which they needed for the rubber tired buggy that struck their fancy. Actually, the law was not aware of Carver.

Wanted were Ben Kilpatrick, six feet tall, 180 pounds, 24 years of age; beard about an inch. Last seen riding an unbranded big, bay horse. George Kilpatrick, 26 years of age, light complexioned, six feet tall, no weight given. Last seen riding a brown horse. Logan—then known as Walker—smaller than the other two. Weight, about 145 pounds, dark complexioned, heavy brown mustache, between thirty-five and forty years of age; bald-headed. Last seen riding a dun horse, branded on left shoulder and left jaw. The Kilpatricks were dressed as cowboys; Logan dresses to kill—like a dude. There were awards out for these to which Concho county added a hundred dollars. The impression at the time was that "Walker" was Carver. This couldn't be for several reasons. Carver wore no mustache nor did he fit the description of the wanted "Walker". Besides, it took more than loud talk to force Carver to draw a six-shooter and it took near killing to force him to use it. He was not violent, ruthless nor brutal but pleasant, cheerful, patient and soft speaking. There are lots of explanations as to why he was with the Black Jack Gang. While the end never justified the means anymore than two wrongs made a right, it is said that he was forced into a killing at a gaming table in San Angelo and fled rather than face the possibility that the Justice of the Peace would not call it self defense. The fact remains that he did join and was with Black Jack before going on to Cassidy. Which causes wonder. Why did he continue after Tom Ketchum was caught. Quien sabe.

Several days after this event Ben Kilpatrick and Will Carver were seen in Sonora, a town of 738 at the time, and ten years the county seat of Sutton county. The stage line ran from Sonora to San Angelo until 1915. The railroad did not come to Sonora until 1913. This visit to Sonora caused the confusion propagated by the press that "Walker" was Carver. On April 1, 1901, despite the fact that they were hunted men, they rode west of Sonora and pitched camp at a water hole of the T Half Circle Ranch.

George Kilpatrick stayed with them possibly because he felt that the law would make him the scapegoat in the Thornton case. He was not known to have ever committed a crime, nor did he ever ride with Black Jack or Cassidy. Ben insisted that his brother was not an outlaw whereupon many shook there heads murmuring that a man was known by the company he kept. On the following day, towards sunset, George Kilpatrick and Will Carver left the water hole and rode into Sonora. Past Mrs. McDonald's Hotel, beyond Mrs. Traweek's boarding house, clear of Hagerland Bros. Mercantile Store, wide away from Meyer Bros. Store, the drug store, the bakery, the post office, barber shop, cantinas over to where some Mexicans had a little settlement—all the time searching for feed for the horses. The little bank suspected a hold-up; people began whispering in the stores. Elijah S. Briant owned the drug store. He was known as "Lige" to the people who frequented his store. Well, here was a case for Lige. Who were those two hombres and what did they really want? Could they be part of the Gang wanted in Concho county for the murder of Thornton? He checked the "Wanted" posters and felt reasonably sure. He suspected that these two had cowboyed for Berry Ketchum in the Devil's River area for they seemed vaguely familiar to him. It was his deputy, a man named Sharp, who made him certain and brought him to action.

Tuesday, April 2, 1901—day of glory for Sheriff Briant; day of doom for William Carver, the only one Detective Dodge recognized in the group picture taken at Fort Worth. On March 19th he had been in Sonora buying horses. Next to money it seemed that the Black Jack Gang and the Wild Bunch loved horses. They tired readily of wine, women and revelry; they struck a bottomless pit when they came to horses. It was love at first sight. The moment they spotted good horse flesh they coveted and sought to possess either through purchase or stealth. In a way fine horses caused their downfall. Wherever they camped, whenever they visited towns, range men, rangers, deputies, sheriffs, detectives wondered about those fine horses. From the time Dodge recognized Carver in the photo they were eventually traced to San Antonio and to Knickerbocker. Every move was watched. It was known that they bought feed there at Tweedy's store; every move they made in and out of camp was observed. No one bothered following the pair to Sonora. They would come back to the camp at the water hole. Anyone could see they planned an indefinite stay. They didn't count on a shortage of feed in Sonora. William and George bought baking powder at the little store kept by a Mexican in the section of town where the Spanish speaking congregated. They asked for grain. He had none for sale. "Try Becketts Livery Stable, senores, he should have some." But he didn't. Next they went to Jack Owen's Bakery for flour and other supplies for their own use. The shop boy was Bossie Sharp who liked to study "Wanted" posters and fancied himself somewhat of a detective. His brother was deputy sheriff. He was certain that Will Carver was one of the men running around in the smart looking buggy that sported rubber tire wheels. This man was wanted for the murder of Thornton. He was so sure of it that he left the store on some pretext, hunted for his brother and insisted that the arrest be made. The reward money would come in handy. Deputy Sharp and Sheriff Briant both agreed that Bossie had a point. They called in Deputy Davis and city lawman W. H. Thompson, walked to the bakery where the sheriff drew on the pair and told them they were under arrest. George, who was nearest the entrance, made a casual effort at compliance; Carver decided to see what he could do with his six-shooter. He had the idea that the slow uplift of hands on the part of Kilpatrick would distract Briant. But the sheriff knew Carver was a deadly shot. While he spoke to George he had concentrated on Will. Before Carver could cock the gun, the sheriff shot. The man in the photo fell to the floor. As

Carver fell Constable Thompson fired at Kilpatrick. Next all four were shooting at the prostrate forms. They must have been scared or were leaving nothing to chance. An interesting sidelight between Carver and Briant reminds one of the gun fight years before near the White Elephant Saloon in Fort Worth, between Luke Short and Longhair Jim Courtright. Like Courtright, Carver's pistol hand, around the thumb and knuckles, was shattered by lead from the sheriff's gun. Like Courtright he tried the border shift but fell to the floor before he could cock the gun. The pair were down but not dead despite the lead poured into them. They were carried to the courthouse, and made as comforable as possible. Carver was given a sedative. In a coma, he re-lived various scenes, yelling:

"Will you stick with me?"

"Will you sweat it out?"

"Die game, boys."

In a moment of consciousness he told the sheriff that he was Will Carver, the range hand known around Sutton County as Cowboy Bill. For a moment he sought to pass himself off as Franks, but too many knew him and he admitted that they were right; he was Carver. He died that night on the floor of the courthouse in Sonora. He had been shot through the right lung, the right leg, hit twice in the left arm, in the hand and near the temple. The surprising thing is that he lived long enough to be carried to courthouse, much less to be able to give his true identity. But is was a night of wonders. George Kilpatrick had fourteen wounds but lived for years to tell the story. Since he was not connected with neither the train robberies nor the murder of Thornton he was given his freedom after serving a short time in jail. He could have made quite a case against Briant or at least Thompson; his wounds were unprovoked. Seems like the four lawmen had a good case of the jitters or followed the old Western idea of shoot first; question later. But that was the way of the transgressor—hardly that of a lawman. A five-thousand-dollar-reward can be mighty tempting money, especially with a "dead or alive" clause.

How the other two back in camp became aware that something was amiss is not revealed. Perhaps the tardiness of the hour or some other reason. Anyway the posse wasn't going out in the dark to round up two men who were expert shots and more accustomed to night shooting than the citizens of Sonora. These two certainly didn't stay around for Carver's funeral. Ben, the Tall Texan, took on the obligation of Laura Bullion, the late Carver's consort. The pair made off to St. Louis and went on a spending spree which did not escape the notice of the ever vigilant city detectives. Mr. and Mrs. Rose were spending much in excess of the salary of a group of cowboys and the lawmen wanted to know why. They tricked Kilpatrick into admitting it was stolen money. Mrs. Rose was picked up at the hotel. Serving a term in prison she vanished from the scene. At the Atlanta penitentiary Kilpatrick abided his time. His debt to society paid, he is again in Texas, in the year 1912.

Terrell county in Texas is a land of creeks and canyons. To the north is the Pecos river; the south marks the international boundary, the Rio Grande, wetback terrain, Big Bend mystery, sparsely settled, a challenge to the onslaughts of civilized society. It is cattle country. The county seat is Sanderson where the people are friendly and welcome a stranger. Very few of those places left —of the old Western hospitality. Southeast of Sanderson are Feodora, Mofeta, Dryden. Dryden named for the chief engineer of the Texas and New Orleans Railroad when the line was surveyed in 1880. In 1912 the population was about one hundred and forty-five. Ida Whitely was post-mistress; B. C. Farley ran a dry goods store. Here was a water tank for the Southern Pacific locomotives. Wednesday evening, March 13, 1912. Number Nine, known as the Sunset limited, stopped for water. Out of the shadows of the night a lone man emerged from hiding in the tall weeds; dry but unbent and defiantly tenacious now that spring was making the rounds again. The masked man was as quiet as an Indian. No one heard him as he approached the train. No one saw him. He tread lightly for a big man. The ground was saturated with moisture about the tank where it lapped up the drippings. The train pulled away from Dryden to make the ascent to Sanderson. Express messenger was preparing the bags, boxes and mail that would be dropped at Sanderson. Engineer turned his head a second. There he stood. The masked bandit, two six-shooters pointed at engineer and fireman. He gave rather a long speech for a hold-up man.

"Stop the train just on the other side of the long trestle. Make sure the front part of the first passenger coach is across on the ground."

The train eased to a stop. Ed Welch, Kilpatrick's companion, climbed aboard with two Winchesters one of which he gave to the Tall Texan. Leaving orders for Welch to keep the men covered Kilpatrick went about getting the baggage car uncoupled. Conductor Henry Erkel hurried forward to investigate. The masked man ordered him to assist brakeman Coskrey in separating the baggage and mail cars from the rest of the train. The undertaking completed, the two trainmen were ordered back into the smoking car—rather poor judgment on Kilpatrick's part to have them out of sight. Ketchum would have told him so, but Tom was long in his grave at Clayton. The postal clerks opened the door at Ben's knock and were ordered to get the door of the express car opened. The first thing he did once he had access to the car was to take the revolvers from the belts suspended on pegs on the wall and toss them out the open door. Had Truesdale and his companion suspected a hold-up the revolvers would have been in their hands. But in 1912 holding up an express car was almost a thing of the past. One would say the exception rather than the rule. Asking

92

the others to stand to one side, Truesdale as messenger was ordered to open the safe. When the messenger told him it was locked it so infuriated Kilpatrick that he shifted the rifle to his left hand and making a fist with his right dealt Truesdale a staggering blow that felled him. Despite the Winchester the messenger sprang to his feet and rushed the bandit who saw him coming. Taking a pistol he buffaloed the game railroad man. Cursing him for a fool he told him to stop his nonsense and open the safe giving him one half minute to make up his mind. "I don't want to kill you unless I have to." And Truesdale knew he spoke the truth. Weak and dizzy he made his way to the safe as the blood coursed down his face. A sack of currency consigned to the bank in Alpine, Texas, containing $60,000 was taken out. The bandit seemed disappointed. He wanted to know where the shipment for El Paso was. Did someone tip him off? How did he know exactly what he wanted? The messenger convinced Kilpatrick that there was no shipment for El Paso but just a sack of cancelled checks going to the Marfa bank. The sack contained about $30,000 in specie. A closer inspection would have revealed the El Paso sack the Tall Texan was after. Truesdale was next ordered to open some registered mail. Kilpatrick took some watches and other valuable articles. Next he ordered the messenger to slit open a sack of onions, spill the contents to the floor and re-fill the sack with the loot. Kilpatrick wanted Truesdale to carry the sack for him as far as the Rio Grande which meant that the bandit hoped to cross the border into Mexico but the messenger wasn't sure whether the desperado would leave him alive at the border. He did some fast thinking. He asked to put on his coat. Turning his back to Kilpatrick he quickly slipped a little cast iron hammer used as an ice breaker into the sleeve and uttered a silent prayer for a chance to use it. Turning to the outlaw he remarked that there was a package in the safe that he overlooked. He took it out of the safe and let it drop between himself and Kilpatrick who placed his Winchester between his knees as he stooped to pick it up. Truesdaye saw the back of his head. He struck twice. Kilpatrick fell on his face. The huddle across the car broke up in a hurry and the outlaw was unarmed in an instant. Truesdale fired two shots to attract Welsh. The messenger used the rifle when Kilpatrick's partner put in appearance. Ben Kilpatrick once associated with the Black Jack Gang died that night. He might have been better off had he remained in the Columbus, New Mexico, jail where he was serving time following the Atlanta stretch. While in jail he grew a beard about a half inch long. It was no longer than that the night he was killed. Evidently Welch was a companion in Columbus where together they worked out the details of this fatal attempt. Perhaps it was Welch who knew about the El Paso shipment. Nineteen years later Truesdale collected the reward. The name Dave A. Truesdale is also found in a number of articles and books dealing with the incident. The bodies of the slain men were taken to Sanderson for burial. No one has disturbed the remains to this day. There are no large posters with arrows pointing to the graveyard; no tourist attraction come-ons as at Fort Summer and Clayton.

The man standing behind the seated Kilpatrick and Cassidy in the famous photo was Harvey Logan, alias Kid Curry, the desperado who had killed Thornton for which Will Carver paid the penalty. He was possibly an inch taller than Carver, long faced, bald, of stocky build, swathy complexion, beady black eyes, could pass for an Indian if he shaved his mustache. He was the fancy one of the lot, always dressed like city-folk. There he drew the line. He was no dandy when it came to guns. Up near the Canadian border in north central Montana on present Highway 2, ten miles from Malta is the little village of Wagner (pop. 50). The Tall Texan and Kid Curry had it comparatively easy setting themselves up in the hide outs from the San Simon valley to the Green river area up to Wyoming where three months and a day (July 3rd) after the death of Will Carver and assisted by Longabaugh, Cassidy, Hanks they held up the train at Wagner. It was Logan who approached the engineer and fireman to command the halting of the train. Cassidy and Hanks kept their Winchesters trained on the passengers. Longabaugh was not his usual quiet self that day. He raced up and down the train waving his pistols shouting at the passengers, raining down threats, making grimaces like a bloodthirsty pirate. But he got results. No one called his bluff. Logan enticed the engineer and fireman to the express car the Winchester doing most of the persuading. The safe was dynamited and the Gang was forty thousand dollars richer. This money (in tens and twenties) was being shipped from the U. S. Treasury in D. C. to the National Bank of Montana in Helena. Reward money totaled ten thousand dollars. No wonder detectives in St. Louis were on the lookout. The money that Ben and Laura (who was with the Tall Texan in Wagner) spent so freely was from this robbery. Thirty-eight year old Hanks of Las Vegas, New Mexico by way of De Witt county, Texas, went his own way after the Wagner hold-up as did Cassidy, Longabaugh, Logan. Logan was shrewed enough to dress and look like a hobo. He sauntered from place to place, cleaning up, dressing up, spending, then a hobo again. By the middle of December he landed in Knoxville, Tennessee. A quick tempered man he buffaloed a man he played pool with because he accused him of cheating. The police were called in to quiet the rumpus only to find that the same pistol that was used to crack a man's skull was now pointed the other way to wound two constables. Although wounded himself, Logan managed to effect his escape, but not for long. In the early fall of that year he was captured and sentenced at Knoxville to serve time in the federal prison at Columbus, Ohio. Now comes the controversy—What happened to him after that? In

95

the summer of the following year he is back in jail at Knoxville. It is said he broke out of jail at Columbus. Whatever the story on June 26, 1903, he slipped a wire over the head of a guard, managed to tie his hands to the prison bars, let himself out of jail fortified with two six-shooters. Outside he found a horse and was gone; no "Wanted" posters would ever help capture him. The nephew of Col. Faucett wrote a book in which he states that "they met an American gunman in Bolivia who went under the name Harvey Logan. Later on the news drifted up from South America that this so-called Kid Curry Gang was wiped out by a bunch of soldiers or rurales when they attempted to hold-up a pay train carrying money for the employees of a tin mine. This occurred at a place called San Vicente." (George S. Fisher-True West Magazine p. 29 December 1956)

Parachute creek rises in north central Garfield county in Colorado and flows southeast into the section of the Colorado river once known as the Blue river. Parachute is a comparatively new name since maps drawn prior to the galloping days of the Black Jack Gang trace the stream but leave it nameless. It received its name because it was within the range of the Naval Oil Shale Reserve that fenced in 67,440 acres. The little settlement at the junction of the two streams is known today as Grand Valley (pop. 209) Here a lone bandit attempted a holdup on July 7, 1903. Crushed by his unsuccessful effort he shot himself to death two days later near Glenwood Springs. The Pinkerton detective Lowell Spence was called upon to identify the body which he emphatically declared to be Kid Curry. This throws out the colonel's nephew's statement that Kid Curry was killed in South America. Actually it was the Sundance Kid who was shot by the soldiers. Several people at Glenwood Springs identified the Grand Valley robber as Tap Duncan who, oddly enough, hailed from Richland Springs and was a relative of the Ketchums. Spence was wrong. He had nothing to substantiate

96

the reason for identifying Duncan as Curry save possibly the hope of scratching Logan off the Pinkerton books. He had been a headache too long. After this Logan disappears. But not to South America. It is my theory that he changed his name and mode of living possibly as a cowboy in some remote region of Utah or Nevada. In 1903 modern methods of police work were coming into play. Carver no doubt had time to see police in action at Knoxville and Columbus. No more train hold-ups for him. Indeed for very few others. All this was now part of the passing parade, the moving scene that bowed out to the racketeer and organized crime. Side arms gave place to shoulder straps, machine guns, hidden weapons. The gunman need no longer face his opponent; gunslingers rode the glory train no more. Trigger fingers were out of style. Knives, blunt instruments, brass knuckles, blackjacks, night sticks, clubs ushered in a new era. Perhaps Carver saw the hand writing on the wall and decided that crime did not pay after all. This change was gradual and years would pass before masked bandits and six-shooters and fast moving horses were to be left to books but automobiles and World War I did hasten the demise of the Kid Curry type of outlaw and desperado.

The Sundance Kid was taller than Butch Cassidy but not as tall as Ben Kilpatrick. He was dark complexioned, long faced, bushy eyebrows, dark brown eyes, cleft or dimpled chin, broad shouldered and brave. What desperado was a weakling? Harry Longabaugh hailed from Sundance, Wyoming, west of Deadwood, South Dakota; cattle country and mining country — the combination loved by those with a flair for six shooters. He was not often associated with Black Jack Ketchum but he was as thick with Butch Cassidy as two peas in a pod. After the Wagner robbery these two went to New York. They had their pictures taken there in the winter of 1901-1902. This may have been their undoing. New York proved unsafe and they booked passage to South America in the nick of time. It is the favorite sport of some authors to dispose of many of such men by saying they went to South America, a distance hardly necessary in prefinger-print, pre-car days. But it made a safe out. However, in the case of the Kid and Butch this was no guess work. They relished the manana tempo. Spanish was not a strange nor foreign language for these two who heard it from infancy. For the next five years they wandered from place to place like two dissatisfied tourists until the spring of 1907 when they obtained employment in the Concordia tin mines in the Santa Vela mountains southeast of La Paz, Bolivia. One may only hazard a guess about those five hidden years. Had they been less lawless and more literary they might have made money writing travelogues, quite the vogue in those pre-World War years. They drew attention to themselves by not wearing side arms in a place where this was the exception rather than the rule. They also proved honest. Sent on an errand for some mules and feed they returned with both the required articles and the change. In their meanderings they had acquired a woman. Two men and a woman had been involved in several bank hold-ups in the Argentine country. Perhaps this told the story of the hidden five years. The moll, incidently, was attached to the Sundance Kid. They met in Denver and the friendship lasted through several of the South American years. It was agreed that she was petite and attractive. What woman with such strange moppets isn't? It has been said that the three settled down to ranch life and had a going concern as stockmen until the Kid was caught with a neighbor's wife by a temperamental husband. The man from Wyoming did not kill him merely wounded him. This ended their country esquire living. On the move again they took a small herd of steers into Bolivia. (See J. D. Horan's ROBIN HOOD IN SOUTH AMERICA THE LAST YEARS OF BUTCH CASSIDY. The Westerners Brand Book N. Y. Posse Vol 1 No. 2)

In time the life in South America was to prove too hectic even for Longabaugh's consort who could never accustom herself to the strange crawling bedfellows usually found in the forsaken spots Butch and Sundance were compelled to use as hideouts. Reptiles and insects were more ghastly than the prospect of capture or sudden death from a six-shooter. The young lady suffered from nostalgia more than other physical airments that induced Longabaugh to bring her back to Denver via New York for medical attention. Either the Pinkerton detectives on the trail were very lax or increasingly indifferent in reaching out for reward money, the Sundance Kid and his lady friend were permitted to go about their affairs unmolested. Taking his consort to the hospital with the promise of visiting her after the operation he went to a cantina with some old cronies and proceeded to hurrah the place in true frontier fashion. He then became involved in some wild shooting at the hotel and evaded capture by jumping on a train for New York where he hid out until he was able to book passage to South America again. That is the story given out about this outlaw up to the year 1908. It seems rather strange for a man as handy with a single action Colt as he was to endanger his life and his freedom every inch of the way from Bolivia to Denver for a woman, yet not go through the only decent thing the woman would expect—marriage. The realization that he had left her on her own in the hospital must have cut deeper than the surgeon's knife.

The end for both Butch Cassidy and the Sundance Kid came in 1909. Let James D. Horan tell it (Westerners Brand Book, Vol. 1 No. 3 p. 21): "The last robbery Cassidy and the Sundance Kid pulled off was the Alpoca Mine hold up. A mule train with the money from the mine, enroute from Alpoca to Tupiza, was held up by two outlaws on a jungle trail. Butch made the mistake of stealing the big silver-gray mule of the mine superintendent. When they rode into a bario in the village of San

Vicente, near Grande river, fifteen miles west of the hold up scene, the hotel owner, also the local Corregidor (constable), spotted the mule and suspected a robbery. While his wife prepared supper for the pair he rode up to contact a small company of Bolivian cavalry ten miles east of La Paz. The soldiers ran out and began shooting from the walls. As twilight deepened into dusk the fire continued. Night fell and the cavalry men threw torches of brushwood into the patio. The flames cast wavering shadows on the wall while a pall of gunpowder smoke hovered over the minature battlefield. They had put their Winchester and extra munitions across the patio and the Kid made one mad dash to try to get it. He picked up the rifle and ran back. Half way across he was shot several times. He died in the dust. Butch saved the last bullet for himself. As the dawn pinked the east the soldiers heard one shot. They later found the western outlaw dead behind their barricade of tables and chairs. The Colt, with its one empty shell, was still in his stiffened hand.'' (Horan o.c.)

It is over. How few the years, how futile the penelope web of time beating those split seconds of darkness brought on by the hangman's mask. Did he think of Sam, Will, Butch, Ben, Harvey in that short yet eternal moment? A dream of seconds spans years of time. This happens in sleep and in moments like this. Because he is on a scaffold the crowd looks up to him, his prison pallor accentuated by the dark clothes, dark mustache, dark eyes. He stands alone, a non-conformist in a quixotic crowd; the only one in that assembly of faces and thoughts and sounds and fury that stands chained yet defiant. They face him—reporters, deputies, thrill seekers—as anxious about his thoughts as he is about the last possible chance of escape. Those who had tickets for the spectacle press close together apprehensive and over-cautious, frightened by every gust of wind, believing in every rumor that mounted riders approached for the sack of Clayton and the liberation of Black Jack Ketchum. The arsenal of their logic is pitted against the potentiality of the daring of Ketchum's friends and the counter bravery of Fort, Garcia and the others who plan to sell their lives dearly in carrying out their instructions. The people have not come to see Ketchum hang. Not really. They came to watch an unrehearsed movie scene, not reel action but real action, and the answer to the question bandied about for weeks—would friends come to the rescue of Black Jack Ketchum? Would the thundering herd from Robbers Roost come riding on the wind in a cloud of dust to stir up ararchy in reckless allegiance to the fallen leader? Thoughts were many that April high noon, and they had too many altercations depending on the side of the fence. Some took a dim view to the hanging; a tolerant view of the one to be hanged. All measured their thoughts in the expectancy of momentary deliverance. The prisoner himself was alert and hopeful despite his merry talk. He looked for the blaze of six-shooters and the smoke of battle once more. Stranger things have happened. He was not awaiting a better world because he never knew a good one. These people did not see a happy warrior who fought for principles built around the pursuant paths of happiness that indulged honor and virtue; his life he lived for Black Jack Ketchum. No one else. Not even a woman. Which is probably why the movies have locked him away in favor of the romantic, less realistic type that would crowd the box office even as the crowd sought tickets to the tragedy on stage at Clayton. Of all the outlaws, train robbers, desperadoes to ride across the pages of truth or fiction in Western six-shooter history, Black Jack Ketchum remains the most indivualistic. His only close friend was himself. His pattern of behavior left no room for anyone but himself. He was his own Robin Hood. He had his moments of kindness as Mary Hudson knew. He was respectful to women; left them alone. People who knew him well testified that he rarely drank, if ever. Writers

101

will insist that he did but that is because they give words ideas rather than rub the dust off the buried words of the past in hidden corners of courthouses, newspaper files, dockets, unattractive attics. Books, in many instances like other products, are made to sell. They depreciate in value like a car. A best seller novel of a few years ago may be found in a second hand store priced down to a few pennies. A rare book would fare no better if it were not for the dealer. The book really has no more value than the day it was printed. It does not add on flavor like old wine. It is the customer who is valuable. Is it important whether or not Ketchum was a drinking man? Billy the Kid was Mc-Carthy or Bonney or Antrim? Does a thing like that change the man? Answer for his deeds or misdeeds? Lessen his skill as a killer or criminal? How many there are who take pride in all they know about Billy the Kid, Butch Cassidy, the Sundance Kid—like an obsession; the truth about these men seems to be more honorable than a tear or sympathetic note for their victims or condolances for the bereaved. It is frightening the amount of space allowed in every Westerners Posse book from coast to coast—to say nothing of all the other books—given over to the glorification of the deeds of the gunslinger, like the sublimation for the killer instinct. More people viewed the body of Killer Cook in Oklahoma than that of General Pershing. If Governor Otero stood on the platform that morning to address the audience how many would have asked for tickets to hear him?

Ketchum was not the type to sit in prison to write his memoirs. His feet were too many years in the stirrup, his hands too often on his guns, his aspirations too readily in money bags. His thinking was blighted by the dreadfully long winter of things hoped for, his own pertinacity chilled by the judgments of men who decreed McGinnis life imprisonment and Black Jack death on the day appointed by the Territorial governor. No dreaming could dull this distressing reality—to die a searcher of the horizon; to hear the murmur of many voices breaking against the scaffold; to be covered by a black sack, the symbol of death—for darkness came even in these last living moments. There was the howl of the wind, dancing over the llano, kicking up dust and suggesting hell. He would keep up a front to the end. A desperado is expected to be brave. So are the virtuous. He was not looking for immortality only a few more years of mortality. To expect death tomorrow and tomorrow. His placid surface covered the fire of the intensity within. While he spoke of hell he really desired to ride the range out of view of the madding crowd, the clamor of voices, the scream of the wind. He was impersonal to the end. So were the people.

CHAPTER FOUR

We would like to think that when the black mask fell over the head and shoulders of Black Jack Ketchum he was as a dying man viewing in a flash the deeds of his life, particularly the last few months from the time he made his insane attempt on the Colorado & Southern. Rather than indulge flights of fancy let us look at the reports the reading public received when all this was going on. Clayton, New Mexico—August 17, 1899—'The southbound C. & S. was held up again last night at the same place as before by one man supposed to have boarded the train at Folsom. Conductor Frank Harrington, who had charge of the train both times before, was in charge and took a shot at the robber with a double barrelled shot gun. After he shot the robber ran. This morning Sheriff Pinard went to the scene of the holdup and found the robber near there badly wounded in the arm. He took the prisoner to Folsom where the doctor picked eleven buckshot out of the wounded man. The identity of the wounded man is unknown. A quantity of dynamite was found at the railroad crossing just in front of the hold up. The railroad authorities wanted to take the prisoner to Trinidad but the sheriff refused to surrender him.''

Denver, Colorado—Same day—''The C. & S. passenger train No. 1 was held up last night near Folsom, New Mexico. The attack occurred at eleven o'clock and was heralded by a fusilade from the bandits. One shot struck mail clerk Bartlett in the jaw and Conductor Harrington was also injured in the arm, but the passengers rallied to the relief of the train crew and the robbers fled. The scene

105

of the attack was within two miles of the scene of the robbery of three weeks ago.''

Trinidad, Colorado—Same day: ''As passenger train No. 1 on the C. & S. was proceeding south between Folsom and DesMoines about 9:30 o'clock last night train robbers attempted to hold up the train but were frustrated in the attempt. The first warning the trainmen had of the attempt was when the engineer was ordered to uncouple the engine and baggage car from the train. The conductor, suspecting trouble, went forward and immediately opened fire on the robber. The hold up man immediately returned fire and shot the express messenger through the left side of the face badly shattering his jaw bone. Frank Harrington, the conductor, also received a very slight wound in the fleshy part of the arm. A special train left Trinidad for the scene of the attempted hold up, and found a man a few rods from the track badly wounded. He asknowledged his name as George Stevens and said that he lived in the Panhandle of Texas. This is the third attempt to hold up the train within two years.''

Black Jack was not recognized because he had grown a three inch beard, had lost much weight especially about the face which seemed thin and haggard when he was caught. This was due in part to the amount of blood he lost during the night he lay so close to the scene of his brush with death. His horse would not let him mount either because he smelled the blood or because Ketchum lacked the strength to control him. The two things Black Jack loved most in life—money and horses—proved elusive that night and betrayed him into the hands of the law. There have been a number of versions regarding the capture of Black Jack Ketchum. One theory is that Conductor Harrington sent word by way of telegraph to Clayton asking that the crew of the freight train several hours behind the passenger known as the Texas Flyer keep a sharp lookout from DeMoines to Emory Gap as he suspected that he had wounded the bandit who may have fallen along the route due to loss of blood. He was fairly certain that the lone robber fled in the night on foot. It was the brakeman perched on the cupola of the caboose who spotted the wounded man several hundred yards from the railroad grade making feeble attempts at waving his cone-like stetson to attract his attention. The engineer, brakeman, fireman went to the wounded man who pointed his six shooter at them and told them to stop where they were. The engineer told him that he had no right to wave them down if he intended to kill them since they stopped at his distress signal. Ketchum agreed that it was better to die in a hospital than out on the lone prairie so he permitted the crew to carry him to the train and rushed him to San Rafael hospital in Trinidad, a rather historic place as one would find by reading Sr. Blandina's AT THE END OF THE SANTA FE TRAIL. At the hospital he submitted to having his beard shaved, but insisted on keeping his bigotes and injured arm. Deputy sheriff G. W. Titsworth, whose son was to write a complete account of his father's part in the capture, induced Ketchum to take "before" and "after" pictures which show him bearded and morose in one while after the shave and bath he posed with a six shooter in his left hand. He wears his big sombrero in both, and is as unsmiling as ever. He doesn't look like a man who knew how to laugh nor cared to if he did.

Santa Fe, N. M. August 21: "The man (George Stevens) who last week attempted to hold up the C. & S. passenger train at Folsom still insists that he had no accomplices in the affair. Stevens would give no clue to his identity more than to state that for some years he had been punching cattle in Texas and New Mexico, and that the last two months he has been placer mining. He says that he had finally determined to make a stake by holding up an express train but as he had failed he is now ready to die. He persistantly refuses to allow his arm be amputated although it is terribly mangled. There is a chance for the man's recovery and the saving of his arm if blood poisoning does not set in. Mail Clerk Bartlett is resting easily and will undoubtedly recover, although he will be disfigured for life. Both men are at Trinidad. It is now believed that Stevens had two assistants who fled when the shooting began.''

Trinidad, Colorado. Same day: ''George Stevens, the bandit wounded in the recent attempt to hold up the C. & S. train near Folsom, N. M., is still in the hospital here, and his condition is most favorable. He got a fairly good night's rest, and was feeling better this morning. But his fever came up this afternoon, however, and he is not so well. Deputy Sheriff G. W. Titsworth, who has guarded the outlaw at night, secured Stevens' consent to have his picture taken. He disliked the idea at first, but after considerable coaxing consented to 'sit.' After breakfast this morning the officer came down town, secured a camera, and got several snap shots of the train robber before and after he had been shaven. Although the officer had only a few minutes instruction in the art, he thinks he got some good photos. No one has as yet identified the outlaw. Many believe him to be the original Black Jack Ketchum, leader of the Hole-in-the-Wall gang of outlaws. (Ketchum repeatedly stated that his men were the Black Jacks. He never alluded to himself as a member either of the Wild Bunch nor the Hole-in-the-Wall Gangs although some of the Black Jacks belonged to both these bands. Nor did news reporters associate Ketchum with any other than the Black Jacks until this time. It is noticeable that the Territorial newspapers and the Arizona papers, with few exceptions, do not refer to Ketchum as the leader of the Hole-in-the-Wall nor the Wild Bunch Gangs, the reference being made by Wyoming, Colorado, Nevada and Utah papers. As a rule when the New Mexico papers do make such reference they are quoting dispatches from these other states. Even Arizona, which vied with New Mexico for the task of hanging Ketchum usually refers to him as the leader of the Black Jacks. This seems to indi-

108

cate that Ketchum was called Black Jack because he was leader of the Gang by that name. We often hear of a man given the nickname of his company, especially if he is the president. When McGinnis was captured the Carlsbad dispatches did not refer to him as a member of the Hole-in-the-Wall Gang but a member of Black Jack Ketchum's Gang. Ketchum said of his men—"They are the Black Jacks.") He had a thoroughbred saddle horse and a pack horse tied a short distance from the scene of the attempted hold-up. The robber says that he is sorry that he shot mail clerk Bartlett. He warned Bartlett three times, he says, to keep his head inside the door, and the fourth time he shot only to frighten the clerk. The bullet struck an iron brace on the door and glanced and struck Bartlett in the jaw. The outlaw seems to have it in for Engineer Kirchgraber and Conductor Harrington. He says that if Harrington had not stepped back in the car he would have 'fixed' him even though his right arm was useless.

"The outlaw is a large, fine looking fellow. He is about six feet one and a quarter inches tall, and about thirty-five years of age. He is dark complexioned, has an intelligent face and a pair of bright, piercing, dark eyes. He still insists that his name is George Stevens."

Again we hit a storm of controversy. Did Ketchum have his arm amputated at Trinidad? Was it Dr. J. R. Espey who admired his courage when he refused an anesthetic, or was it the doctor in Santa Fe? Was the arm removed at all? It's just like saying Garrett did not kill Billy the Kid. Years ago when I talked to one of the men who carried the Kid's body to the grave, he stated emphatically that it was the notorious outlaw who had escaped the Lincoln jail. In going over material to aid in putting this book together I came across a statement to the effect that many believe that Ketchum had his arm amputated but he didn't. B. D. Titsworth says Trinidad is the place; Otero (who was also in position to know) says Santa Fe. Thompson, the last man to interview Ketchum, was definite about an armless sleeve. All the evidence points to Santa Fe as the place. After all, what difference did it make to the man on the scaffold waiting for the hatchet to descend on the rope. Jerome, Arizona, August 26: "The man who attempted to hold-up the express train near Folsom, New Mexico, on the night of August 16th, and was wounded and later captured, has been identified by the officers of this county (Yavapai) as the Camp Verge murderer and a requisition was made today for his return to Arizona. The accused proves to be Black Jack, who is now in the hands of the U. S. officers at Santa Fe, New Mexico. When captured, Black Jack had the hand made purse, .45 Colt Revolver, and when his saddle and pack horse were found, the saddle and blanket described minutely by those at the scene of the crime. The officers state that the identification is firmly established . . . "

Santa Fe, August 23rd: "U. S. Marshall Foraker will arrive in this city tonight with two train robbers (McGinnis was brought to Trinidad from Carlsbad. It was probably he who told Tom Ketchum that Sam was dead. Black Jack no doubt learned in the hospital of Sam's attempt on the train just a few weeks before his own) having come by Trinidad to bring George Stevens, or as some believe the original Black Jack who was wounded in the latest attempt to rob a train at Folsom. When he was wounded he had a pair of thoroughbred horses tied a short distance from the scene of the hold-up. . . ." It then repeats how sorry he is for hurting Bartlett and how he would like to get his hands on Kirchgraber and Harrington. It also adds—"From the very first he contended that he would not permit an arm to be amputated, and it has not been done. When told that he would likely die unless the arm was removed, he cooly replied, 'Let death come.' With reference to the identification of McGinnis (the other robber) the marshall is bringing from Carls-

110

bad, it is learned that J. K. Hunt, the Cimarron merchant who recognized the prisoner, had feared the men meant to hold up his store. He noted their movements carefully, taking a minute description of the men, their outfit and horses. They were in his vicinity about three weeks. When the train was held up he gave a description to the officers. The only point which did not tally with Hunt's description was the weight of the prisoner. At Cimarron he weighed one hundred and seventy-five pounds; at Carlsbad only one hundred and forty-five. This is explained however, by the fact that he (McGinnis) had ridden over four hundred miles, suffering with four wounds, and certainly agony keen enough to reduce him in flesh. The officers greatly regret the escape of Franks, the prisoner's partner, as he is regarded as an even more important man McGinnis, being considered the leader of the Gang, ranking Ketchum. Franks was the man who directed operations and cursed Ketchum and McGinnis roundly for the manner in which they delayed matters. He was in a towering rage and told them they didn't know enough to rob an ox train. He understood the handling of dynamite, personally blowing open the express safe of the Southern. It is believed that he was the man who killed Sheriff Farr and wounded Smith and other members of the posse at the Cimarron fight. At the time that McGinnis was captured Franks was away from camp hunting horses. He returned while the fight was in progress, but seeing that the battle was going against his partner, watched it from a hill half a mile away, and at the end of it waved his hat to the officers and galloped off. Sheriff Stewart had a wounded man to care for, and was delayed in taking a train until ten hours later. He followed in pursuit about two hundred and fifty miles, but now knows that Franks doubled on his tracks at Seven Rivers, seventeen miles north of town, giving him the slip. It is now said the two men were contemplating a raid on the bank at Carlsbad. They have been in town four successive nights

111

planning the attack. There is a reward of $1,400 for the men which will be paid to Sheriff Stewart immediately on the conviction of McGinnis.''

Santa Fe, August 25th ... They (sheriff and marshall) also brought with them Tom Ketchum, one of the men who recently attempted to hold up a train and the C. & S. and was shot by Conductor Harrington. Tom Ketchum is badly wounded on the right arm by eleven buckshot from the gun of the conductor. It is feared that blood poisoning has set in and that he will die the same as his brother Sam did at the penitentiary, from a wound in the shoulder, a short time ago. Sheriff Stewart after assisting in delivering the two men at the penitentiary left last night for Eddy county. Tom Ketchum was taken in charge by Marshall Foraker at Trinidad, where the outlaw was in the hospital. Ketchum refused to have his arm amputated and attempted suicide. He first asked for a revolver with which to shoot himself and when this was refused, took the bandages from his arm when alone and wrapped them around his neck, put his foot into the loop, trying to strangle himself. He was unconscious when found, and it was two hours before he regained consciousness. At first he was sullen and surly, but later became talkative and told Marshall Foraker that he had committed a number of robberies, but was not with his brother when the recent train robbery near Folsom was committed. In fact, he did not know that his brother was dead (?) until Marshall Foraker told him 'If I had known that the train had been held up near Folsom only a short time before, I would not have made an attempt a second time,' Ketchum told Foraker.

''Marshall Foraker is convinced that Ketchum is the original Black Jack. Ketchum at first gave his name as George Stevens. He said when arrested that the affair at Folsom was his first attempt at train robbing and that formerly he was a peaceable cowboy, and was alone in the hold-up. But he admitted later having accomplices in the last hold-up at Folsom.

"Both prisoners were given a hearing this afternoon at the penitentiary by U. S. Commissioner J. P. Victory. The prisoners waived examination to the nominal charge of interfering with the U. S. Mails and were asked to furnish $1,000 bond for their appearance at court. More serious charges will be made later. It is related that the brother of the Ketchum at San Angelo, Texas, some months ago supplied Tom and Sam with money to start the cattle business in Idaho. The two brothers afterwards separated and independently sought their old stamping ground in northeastern New Mexico and without knowledge of each other resolved to rob the Colorado & Southern train, upon different occasions, and both met with disaster."

Jim Hunt, who later gave up his store at Cimarron to take over the Raton Range newspaper, insisted that George Stevens was Black Jack Ketchum. Word was sent to Tom Green county in Texas to have some one come to Santa Fe for the purpose of identifying the prisoner. G. W. Shields, the sheriff, who had known Tom all his life and often hunted and fished with him when they were boys came to the capital and identified Tom as his former playmate. He had with him Bige Duncan of Knicker-bocker, Ketchum's brother-in-law. Duncan said little but was obviously upset for the family had hoped that the two brothers were in Idaho outfitting a spread as cattle-men. When Tom saw Duncan and Shields he broke down and wept bitterly, one of the few times he displayed any emotion. Tom's sister had often pleaded with him to abandon his ways and walk the straight and narrow. It was more for her sake that he accepted the money from Berry. No doubt his intention was good so long as he remained about Knickerbocker with his sister's restrain-ing influence to guide him. Centuries before it was writ-ten: "The spirit is willing but the flesh is weak." Once on the road north Tom reverted to his former self. This does help to account for some of his time prior to the second train robbery when the brothers parted forever. Rumor has it that Ketchum mentioned a three hundred page manuscript about himself and his crimes written while awaiting execution. Should this document have been a reality Otero would have known about it. So far it has never come to light. There is a possibility that it was taken to Knickerbocker with the personal effects of Tom after he was hanged. Naturally the family would burn it without even bothering to read it. While confession is good for the soul, written confessions had best be destroyed because of the curious. The good in a man should live after him; the other should be interred with his bones. When Tom was leaving Trinidad for Santa Fe a crowd of eight hundred men, women and children milled about the depot for a glimpse of him. In proportion to the population of Trinidad at the time this constituted quite an assembly. Some so-called stars in Hollywood would have envied Tom. Ketchum refused to satisfy or gratify the morbid curiosity of the crowd unless they took up a collection for the privilege of seeing his handsome face. McGinnis, since there was nothing physically wrong with him, was taken to the station in a closed carriage. He absolutely refused to pose for a photograph but did make some remarks about his fight with the posse near Carlsbad. While the crowd got a good look at him it would have been happier if the wind or somebody had knocked Ketchum's big sombrero off his face as he lay there in the open wagon. Shields claimed that his first arrest as sheriff in 1888 was Tom Ketchum who shot a dog around the church while people were at worship. He also said that he had spent about three thousand dollars since 1893 looking for Tom. Perhaps. This may be paper talk since both Ketchums were home often enough between crimes if sheriffs, deputies, detectives wanted them bad enough. Publicity makes heroes of unknowns overnight. What would be the written word if after all the sheriffs and lawmen like Earp, Masterson, Stewart and others were confronted with the outlaw's version of the case in question? While the desperado deserves punishment one would be interested in his motives even though we do not justify them. Billy the Kid is glorified; so is Pat Garrett. Which side of the fence then, is anybody on? "That is Billy the Kid. Woh!" "That is Garrett who killed Billy the Kid. Woh! Later Garrett knows enough about the Kid to write his life. But the Kid is not around to write the life of Garrett. A number of lawmen have told their deeds in print. Were they trying to prove to themselves how great they were? Or merely leaving footprints on the sands of time? Deeds speak for themselves. Future generations will merit or demerit as they sit in judgment. Truth has a way of devouring legend even if it takes centuries. The sheriff bet a box of cigars that Tom would never be hanged. He woul 1 commit suicide or permit himself to be shot in an atte.npted escape. Perhaps he won that bet. Ketchum was not hanged in the sense of results for his neck was not broken. He was decapitated. He committed suicide in that last fatal plunge. Duncan spoke of Berry and Mrs. Duncan; thus we may assume that the parents of the Ketchums were dead and spared the anguish felt by the son and daughter when they learned their plans for making ranchers out of Tom and Sam went awry. Tom needed help. His thinking was wrong. A phychiatrist or a spiritual advisor may have been the answer to his warped idea that nothing could be done for him since he was singled out for hell. This seems to be the cut and the answer for his life of crime. Also for Sam's. The enjoyment of life, plenty of money, no work, no tying oneself to a wife and family. No matter which way he flipped the coin he was condemned. So thought Tom. His words and actions indicated this as his way of thinking. Many others have thought that way without outlawing themselves against society.

Santa Fe, N. M. September 4, 1899: "Yesterday Sheriff G. L. Murdo of Prescott, Arizona, came to this city to have a look at Tom Ketchum the wounded robber at the penitentiary for whom he had been hunting for the past two months. At Camp Verde some months ago Ketchum killed two merchants and wounded a third man while seeking to rob a store. According to the sheriff Ketchum was one of several men sitting upon the porch of the store when darkness came. One of the proprietors went inside to close up for the night. Ketchum asked what he wanted in for. The other merchant explained and asked him whether he wanted anything. Ketchum directed him also to enter. He obeyed and Ketchum followed. The man started to run through the store but was pursued and as he entered a rear room where there was a lighted candle near the safe. Ketchum placed a revolver at the head of the fugitive, who fell dead, his neck broken by the bullet. The partner ran for the front door, and fell outside dead from a bullet fired by Ketchum. A man started to pick up the body when Ketchum declared he would kill all of them while he was at it, firing a third shot, which wounded one in the leg. For some reason, however, the robber ran away. Rewards for his arrest and conviction amount to $2,300. The Arizona sheriff, Munds, has been searching for Ketchum ever since and had a posse with him in the Datil mountains in Socorro county when he found a paper at a sheep ranch which told of the arrest of the man wanted in Arizona. He promptly came to this city to ascertain whether the prisoner was the one for whom he had been looking, and found this to be the case. Should the charge against Ketchum of robbing the train be waived by the Territory, and the complaint against him by the government of interferring with mails be withdrawn the outlaw could be taken to Arizona and convicted for murder. As Ketchum was apprehended before a reward for his last criminal act, it is likely that the officers can secure no reward unless it be the amounts offered in

Arizona. Convictions for earlier crimes in New Mexico might not result from trials, as witnesses could not now be found, perhaps, unless it should be in the case of the murder of the postmaster at Liberty. Ketchum's condition yesterday following the amputation of his arm was satisfactory to the surgeons. McGinnis, the other robber at the prison, is non-communicative.''

Ibid. ''Tom Ketchum is reported to be rallying. His recovery seems to be certain, and is attributed by the physician to the fact that he never in his life has touched a drop of alcoholic liquors, and even refused alcoholic stimulants after the operation.''

Santa Fe, October 2, 1899: ''When Sheriff Stewart of Eddy county called on a wounded man in the hospital a few days ago Black Jack said jocosely to the sheriff, 'I'm getting fat so that when they hang me they can eat me if they want to.' Secretary Martin was present and after leaving the hospital concluded that there was 'something up' to lead the prisoner to talk in such a tone and told the sheriff that Ketchum was planning to escape. After a report on this subject was made to Superintendent Bursum, special vigilance was exercised, with the result that a plan to secure the escape of the train robber was discovered. In the clothes used as a bandage for the wound of the prisoner and wrapped around his body was found a steel saw made of a clock spring apparently, and in the water closet of the hospital, which the prisoner frequents, a complete wooden pistol covered with tinfoil was discovered hidden. The plan contemplated was to saw through the hospital's floor, surprise a guard by flourishing the mock weapon, seize the guard's gun and fight a way out if necessary, or perish in the attempt. There is no doubt that the prisoner is quite equal to a bold attempt of this character. When the saw was discovered on the person of the convalescent, he broke down with emotion. He was promptly removed from the hospital to the cell house, from which he cannot hope to escape. That the convict had

117

confederates in making these preparations goes without saying. But who they are and whether they are known is not now given out. That there are outsiders ready to spend money to secure the release of the robber is known, and some one has retained attorneys to defend the other highwayman, McGinnis, who has been taken to Raton for trial. Ketchum has a rich brother, and the bandit's companions on many raids are interested in helping the man to escape. The vigilance of the officers probably has prevented a tragedy in or about the hospital, but now that the prisoner has been placed in a cell no possible scheme can avail him.''

Santa Fe, November 10, 1899: ''The U. S. Department of Justice, through the U. S. District Attorney W. B. Childers, has given the authority to send the necessary papers authorizing the removal of Tom Ketchum to Yavapie county, Arizona, for trial on charge of murder, with the understanding that should he be acquitted or sentenced only to a term of years he should be brought back to be tried on the charges that the U. S. has brought against him. Judge McFie, as Judge of the U. S. District Court, has countersigned the proper orders providing the delivery of Ketchum to an Arizona official who is expected to arrive here tomorrow morning. A difficulty however has arisen which may prevent the delivery. Ketchum is also under indictment by a Territorial Grand Jury in Union county for a capital offense, and, unless Governor Otero honors the requisition papers of the Governor of Arizona which the Arizona official will probably present to him Ketchum will not be taken to Arizona.'' Ibid. ''Today (Nov. 1) Governor Otero considered the requisition of the Governor of Arizona for the delivery to that Territory of Tom Ketchum the train robber. Sheriff Munds of Yavapica county came to the capital as the agent for Arizona. Ketchum, in cold blood, killed two merchants in that county, and, when captured in New Mexico was being sought by the Arizona sheriff. There were rewards offered in Arizona for the arrest and conviction of the assassin amounting to $2,300. A large part of the sum was to be given for the apprehension of the fugitive, dead or alive. Ketchum was wounded in attempting to rob a train near Folsom, picked up by the wayside and identified by the trainmen. He was turned over to the U. S. Marshall of New Mexico and held to answer for unlawfully interfering with the transmission of mails by stopping the train. Later, indictments were found against him by the Territorial courts for trying to rob trains in more than one instance, and indictments will be found against him for the murder of a postmaster and several other men at Liberty, Union county, in company with his brother, who recently died in the penitentiary from a gunshot wound received in the act of robbing a train. The Arizona authorities secured the consent of the Department of Justice to waive its prior right to try Ketchum for interfering with the mails in order that he might be taken first to Arizona and tried for murder, where execution would certainly result. In the meantime charges against him in New Mexico had taken the form of indictments and the consent of the Territory had to be asked for in order to transfer him to Arizona as he is also a Territorial prisoner. This matter was submitted to Governor Otero. District Attorney Leahy of Raton resisted the requisition, assisted by District Attorney Gortner on behalf of Soliciter General Bartlett. Section 115 of the Compiled Laws of New Mexico provides that any person who makes an assault on a train or upon passengers or employees of a train for the purpose of robbery as did Ketchum when he wounded several trainsmen is guilty of a felony, the penalty for which is death. Otero refused to honor the request of Governor Murphy because he wished to uphold Leahy. He also wished to prove to the rest of the nation that New Mexico was perfectly capable of handling its outlaws and he wished to make an example of

119

Ketchum in order to prevent further trouble along this line."

Governor W. L. Thornton wrote to the Department of Interior, September 21, 1893: "There is only one other act of the last legislature that requires notice, and that is the one creating Union county out of parts of Colfax, Mora, and San Miguel counties. This act does not go into effect until January 1, 1894. It takes eighty-one townships off the eastern part of Colfax county; forty-five from eastern Mora county, and about forty townships from the northeastern corner of San Miguel county. It will occupy the extreme northeastern portion of New Mexico."

Stephen W. Dorsey was U. S. Senator from Arkansas from 1873 to 1879. He had a ranch at Chico Springs east of Springer in New Mexico. His range manager was John C. Hill who thought that a town should be founded on the new line of railway then building across Dorsey's vast domain in northeastern New Mexico. General Dodge, owner of the new line, was in favor of the idea and a townsite company was formed, the site chosen and named Clayton to honor Clayton C. Dorsey, the former senator's son. Hill was the moving spirit of the Clayton Land and Investment Company. Charles M. Perrin surveyed the line for the railroad from Trinidad to Texline; Thomas S. Holland platted the site. After all this the townsite company began to wonder whether or not it was able to obtain a clear title for the proposed city. The railroad built through unoccupied government domain. Prompt ownership to this land was merely a matter of filing land script on it. Land script was mostly for the benefit of veterans of the Indian Wars, Civil War and service men in general. Congress passed an Act whereby a man in uniform who sought title to his quarter-section might obtain enough script to supply for a deficiency should any occur. This could be applied on untenanted, unclaimed Federal land and did not require residence on the part of the soldier. This acquisition was known as

120

Soldiers Additional Script. A former serviceman in Missouri (Simon Shaddox) owned the spot Hill and the townsite company sought for the Clayton development. The company was able to acquire the land from Shaddox, at leat forty acres of it, despite the fact that the town was already a reality before the actual Patent was received in December of 1891. In fact the postoffice for a time was known as Perrico. Here Tom Ketchum received his mail in the early days when he trailed cattle for the PCC outfit.

The townsite was laid out in February 1888. The first train entered the new city (mostly of tents then) on March 20, 1888. The usual frontier element infiltrated—cowboys, sheep ranchers, cattlemen, gamblers, gunslingers, grisettes, bartenders, dance hall girls, lawyers, cooks, barbers. The first live stock agent for the railroad was James C. Leary, once a cowboy for Senator Dorsey. The Clayton stockyards were completed in August of 1888. Leary now worked to step up the Pecos valley trade. Taking Hill along with him he loaded a buckboard with supplies and brandy that was first cousin to Taos Lightning known as Cedar Valley Bourbon, sold by the former Texas Ranger Captain McMurray, he headed for the little hamlet of Roswell even then the center of the Pecos valley trade. Leary and Hill stopped at every ranch along the way and extolled the glories of Clayton. They had plenty of competition. Drummers from the new villages of Amarillo, Canadian, Pampa were also working in opposition to Clayton and the little chamber of commerce did not fare as well as they had hoped. A trail herd numbered up to eighteen hundred cattle. This was in the days when white faces were beginning to surplant the longhorn and other breed found on the plains. O. H. Nelson had introduced Herefords to this section about 1882.

Going to the postoffice today in the ultra modern city one would hardly believe that here a dry lake filled with water in the spring and summer drew chuck wagons and campsites during those pioneer days, while the cattle were always kept at the cow camp as far as twenty miles from town, the horses were often led to this lake to quench their thirst. Black Jack was seen here on occasion when engaged in the carefree pursuits of cowboying. The chute at Clayton was often the scene of the bloody operation of sawing off the long horns of the cattle to facilitate shipment. During those trail-riding days as many as fifteen separate outfits, each with its quota of cowboys, camped about Clayton at one time. Often it would be six weeks before a shipment was ordered. This meant that the boys got together often to hurrah the town. Dance halls, gambling places, amourettes, and saloons, about a half mile from the center of town were frequently visited and six week romances were neither the exception nor the rule. Pay day. That was the day. Monte, poker, liquor, women. The cowboy returned to Pecos valley none the worse for wear.

The first building put up in Clayton was that occupied by Charles M. Perrin, originally his business house, later his residence. The lumber was bought from Thomas O. Boggs an old frontiersman who took Kit Carson's children as his own when the old scout passed away. Boggs had a sheep ranch on the Pinavetitos. Since he now made Springer his home he sold his corrals, sheds, outhouses to Hill. These were taken apart board by board and became the skeletons of some of the first buildings in Clayton. Two of such buildings were saloons. Before long the first unit of the townsite was enlarged through acquisitions from four additional land entries filed upon by Marcellus D. Harrison, Hill, Henry Hayes, Cage and Perrin. George W. Benton established the Clayton Enterprise. Homer E. Byer was postmaster. Hill was first Justice of the Peace but later resigned in favor of Col. Love. Benton sold his paper to Curren.

"Our town which started a little over a year ago has grown slowly but its growth was sure. We are the supply point for one hundred miles north and south; we have three of the best, cheapest and most reliable mercantile houses in the Territory. We have also two excellent hotels, and our postoffice is a money-order office, too. It does more business than any of the size in the county. We possess a fortune in the most wonderful climate on earth. We have an excellent school taught by an Eastern college graduate. Two clergymen point out to us the straight and narrow way and the same number of skilled physicians take care of our sick. Our real estate is advancing rapidly in price, each week seeing some of our town property changing hands. But we still have needs, among others, a bank. A lawyer we would welcome and have no doubt he would build up a good practice at once ... Of course Clayton had its period of excitement such as shooting scrapes caused by gamblers and toughs who wanted to run the town. All new towns in the West must pass through such experiences as certainly as teething and measles fall to the lot of children. That time has expired during the early infancy of the town, and now it would be hard to find a more quiet and law abiding place than it is.'' (*Enterprise* May 4, 1889)

"We have two two-story hotels. Several dwelling houses, all good, and some of the most sightly architecture and goodly dimensions. Three stores of general merchandise, each doing a good business. A banking business has lately been added to one of them. While that of Fox Bros., Bushnell & Co. average monthly sales of $8,000 which fact alone proves the prosperity of the town. One drug store is here. It would do a better business were it located in a less healthy community. A newspaper, a school house and a church are also here . . . Here too, is found the saloon. The saloon business has fallen off in the past two months. During the early days there were no less than eleven saloons, but as the railroad came and pursued its way north eight of these followed the road. A wool house one hundred feet long is built and from it was shipped

483,000 lbs. of wool last season. Last fall there were 50,-000 and 60,000 cattle shipped from this point. J. C. Hill beginning as a cowboy, now at the age of thirty finds himself president of one of the largest and best of the New Mexico cattle companies, owning the controlling interest in his company.'' (Ibid)

''On the last Sunday of March, 1890, Charles Merideth killed 'Red' Dent Kyes, his partner in the Favorite Saloon. Charles and Red were good friends. Red was employed by the Home Land Office & Cattle Co. He saved his money and bought one half interest in the cantina. On the evening of this particular Sunday both partners were behind the bar when they began an argument over some trivial matter. One word led to another and before long they were shouting at each other. Merideth thought Red threatened him and reached for his gun beneath the counter. Red, seeing his partner's action, went for his own gun and before he could bring it into play Merideth's gun was smoking. Two shots caught Red in the right lung. Mortally wounded Red fired four shots aimlessly. Of the seven shots fired only two took effect. Red was carried to the drug store but nothing could be done for him. He died Monday afternoon.'' There is a story told that Dorsey wrote out the funeral oration and Mrs Hill delivered it. Actually Rev. S. A. Dyson conducted the funeral. Merideth was exhonorated. All of Clayton turned out for the funeral as Red was quite popular. (See the account the Colfax County Criminal and Docket book)

In 1891 T. E. Gibbons became station agent; A. W. Thompson postmaster and later editor of the paper; George A. Bushnell and H. E. Byler notary publics; W. A. Pender carpenter, contractor, builder; B. McGovern barber and hair dresser (his shop was in the rear of the Favorite Saloon); Young & Merideth ran the Clayton Hotel; Young had the Blacksmith and Wagon Shop; Dodson ran a shoe store.

"Clayton has no deputy sheriff, neither do we have a constable, or a road supervisor for this precinct, and if the County Commissioners don't soon furnish the Justice of the Peace with a docket book in which to docket his cases, he threatens to resign."(*Enterprise,* April 25, 1891)

"Clayton is still in the hands of desperadoes and is in need of deputy sheriffs every day. Horse thieves steal horses from hitching posts in front of the stores and along the streets of the town. One merchant who presented a bill to one of the cowboys for a saddle came near perforated for asking him to pay for the goods while the constable who tried to make the arrest was compelled to dance to the music of the six-shooter. The citizens are unable to do anything and Sheriff Stockton, for some reason, still refuses to secure deputies enough to protect the town and that part of the country from ruffians." (*Folsom Metropolitan,* Sept 19, 1891)

Porter and Denton were two desperadoes from Clayton. Porter was even tougher than Black Jack Ketchum but did not capture the imagination nor the fancy of the public as the train robber. Tucked away in the county jail at Springer Porter spent his time thinking up avenues of escape. He worked on a dummy. In the jail at the same time were Denton, who helped with the deception, Francisco Lucero of Trinidad who killed a man in the Buena Vista section of Raton, E. Arguello who killed Asher Jones, James Gibbons indicted for murder. The substitute jailor took very little time out for sleep. Borrowing clothing from his cell mates Porter fixed up a prone figure and told Denton to call to the jailor that Porter was ill. The jailor refused to bite. At dinner time, bothered by his conscience for his hardness, he decided to fix a special lunch for the sick man, carrying the tray to him personally. Porter was secreted behind a cage. When the jailor neared the sick man's cot, he jumped out the door, threw back the lever opening the cell doors and the prisoners rushed out. Together they overpowered the jailor, bound him hand and foot gagged him and gave him the place of the dummy. Denton and Porter suggested that the jailor carry out a basket of scrapes that was in the far corner of the cage. Denton secured a pistol, hustled Colly into a cell, barred the door and walked out. The jailor was later rescued by Elbert Harmon. A posse took after the fugitives who had divided in pairs. The constable (Trujillo) decided to continue after Porter and Denton. Their trail led to the railroad track above town and then up the track some distance beyond the stock yards where at a small bridge either Denton or Porter left a shot gun stolen from the jail. Here the trail left the railroad and took the direction of the old ford of the Red River. Ten minutes later the escapees were surrounded and brought back to jail. The others were apprehended at the Trujillo ranch just south of the Gonzolez mesa. Harmon and Trujillo were given fifty dollars each by the county for their work. (See: *Clayton Enterprise,* Sept. 19, 1891)

"Owing to the dereliction of our sheriff in not appointing a deputy for Clayton, the best and only way left to enforce law and order in eastern New Mexico is for our citizens to get a constable appointed for this precinct and then let the citizens contribute a small amount additional for the building of a calaboose and the maintenence of the constable. As it is now no man will act as constable for what there is in it, and the J. P. cannot enforce the laws without assistance. That funny man-roping scene which occurred on our streets last week out-rivaled the reckless scenes of Dodge City in its worst days and while the man who was roped might have deserved what he got, that does not mitigate or justify such lawless actions. The question is this: Do we want to make a town at Clayton where our wives and families can live without fear of danger or insult, or do we want to make it a rendezvous for the toughs and hard characters of the frontier?

126

"That is the question. We called a meeting of the citizens together last week to take some action on this matter but owing to a conflict of opinion no definite plan was agreed upon. Some favored the establishment of a committee to report violations of the law to the grand jury, while others favored hiring a man to act as deputy sheriff in connection with a regular appointment, while still others said they had good sixshooters and Winchesters to defend themselves, and, by the eternal, they proposed to do so. But all this does not satisfy the demand of law and order and it is very foolish for any man to think he is stronger than the law. The law is stronger than any man, and we have good laws in New Mexico but the great trouble lies in the immediate execution of them. The only way to enforce them with advantage to the local communities is to catch the violator of the law right in the act or beginning and place him in the calaboose. Ninety-nine percent of the men who shoot up our small towns first get boisterously drunk, then follows murders, ropings and serious criminal offenses. If the man who was roped last week had been arrested and placed in a calaboose in the beginning of his wild and profane career it would have saved Clayton the greatest stigma she has ever known.

"Some of our citizens suggested reporting violators to the grand jury but we are not in favor of this plan because a crazy drunken man cares nothing at all for all the grand juries on earth. He is now c.m. and knows nothing except to terrorize the town and to be a 'bad man' generally and a first class bad man gets away from the grand jurors. It is only the best class of criminals that are overtaken by the grand juries of this Territory and then they usually get out of jail in a few months and come back and 'lay' for the man who reported them. No, what we need is a good, cool, nervy, constable or deputy sheriff who is not a professional killer or rowdy but who is a gentleman with all that: One who can walk up to a bunch of cowboys

127

and say, 'Boys, please take off your six-shooters while in town,' and see that they do so. If a man is drunk or disorderly put him in the calaboose until he cools off. Therefore, seeing as our county seat is too far away. (The county seat changed places many times—E Town, Cimarron, Springer, Raton—this latter being the county seat when Union county was formed and Clayton became the county seat of the new county.), and our sheriff will not appoint a deputy sheriff for unknown reasons, we would suggest that all citizens who are in favor of law and order and the protection of life and property do, at once, contribute a small amount monthiy toward the support and maintenance of a good constable or deputy sheriff and the building of a calaboose as the proven steps to enforce law and order along this line. *THE CLAYTON ENTERPRISE* will head the list with ten dollars per month every month to defray the additional salary of the said officer and the building of the calaboose. (August 1, 1891)

But the cowboys still came in to dance with Box Car Alice, Coon Ida, Queen Bess and others who knew how to draw them out of their loneliness and their money. From October 30 to November 17, 1889 all communication between Clayton and the outside world was cut off because of a blizzard. Henry Miller, John Martin, Charles Jolly and two other cowboys perished in this storm. The first school teacher was Ida Cavanaugh of Las Vegas who filed a homestead just west of town where she built a small cottage during her teaching days. When she married Col. John Love, Ward W. Savery, a Yale graduate (class of 1883) became Clayton's second school teacher. Thomas Smith, Chief Justice of the Territory of New Mexico was the first judge to hold District Court in Clayton, September 1st, 1893. He was succeeded by W. J. Mills in 1898. It was Mills who presided during the Ketchum trial. Narciso Faustin Gallegos was District Court interpreter for Judge Mills as well as for Judge Smith, serving from

128

1893 to 1900. J. S. Holland wrote to Governor Thornton August 12, 1896:

"Our people are turning their attention to agriculture and are raising vegetables enough for home consumption. Quite a number have built reservoirs and planted alfalfa, and in the future will fatten their sheep and cattle at home. The cattle companies who formerly held control of our grazing lands have given way to actual settlers with small herds, who are breeding up their herds and will soon have a better class of cattle. This section is a paradise for sheep, and I suppose we have more sheep in this county than in any other section of the Territory, and more of them are improved Merinos, while some sheep men have imported Shropshires, and they seem to do well. Our people are beginning to learn that protection on wool does not protect, and that supply and demand control the prices. We have some good prospects for coal near Clayton, but so far they have not been developed. Clayton has a new schoolhouse which cost $10,000, and we expect to get an appropriation from the next session of the legislative assembly. Our labor supply is equal to the demand. We have three public buildings in the county—Clayton schoolhouse ($10,000) Union county courthouse and jail ($19,-000). They are large and commodious and are well kept and in good condition. We have no Indians. The production of lumber is small."

Several years after the Black Jack trial Clayton is to get a new $50,000 courthouse and jail. Ketchum was brought for trial to the $19,000 courthouse. The population then was about 700. William B. Bunker a lawyer from Las Vegas was named to conduct the defense. Jeremiah Leahy of Raton was prosecuting attorney. Ketchum thought up several schemes for escape; none of them worked. He told Dr. Sloan at the penitentiary where he and his brother had hid money. The doctor's search proved fruitless just as the prisoner expected. By appealing to the governor the doctor hoped to obtain permission to take Ketchum with him to Tom Green county in Texas where the treasure was supposedly hidden. The plan failed. All during the trial at Clayton Ketchum still hoped. He despised Frank Harrington and often expressed regret that he didn't finish him off at the hold-up. Kirchgraber he "hoped to see in hell." It was the first time that Ketchum was involved in a trial by jury. He was visibly impressed, often looking at the audience to see if he could recognize anyone. Drew, Kirchgraber, Harrington and several other witnesses left the jury no choice: "We, the jury, in the case of the Territory of New Mexico vs. Thomas E. Ketchum—find the defendant guilty in the manner and form charged in the indictment. We fix the punishment at death." Ketchum seemed to expect the verdict. He looked at Judge Mills, turned to Leahy, then to the people but said nothing nor gave any indication that the verdict affected him in any way. He was brought back to his cell in the Clayton jail. Nobody seemed concerned that he would escape or that others would help him escape. Papers took no further notice of him until a day or two prior to the execution. Ketchum was sentenced to be hanged on October 4, 1900. The indictment was Territorial—His offense against the Territory of New Mexico. For this reason he was brought back to Santa Fe and known as No. 132. Bunker asked for a stay of execution and sought to appeal the case. Leahy would have none of it. Otero decided to give Bunker a chance to produce new evidence. Meaning the hanging was delayed until March 27, 1901. Failing in this the governor set the day for the execution. April 26, 1901. In prison Ketchum ate well, was particularly fond of candy and peanuts. The inactivity brought a pallor to his cheeks but also puffed them to fullness. He was a good deal heavier on the scaffold than during the trial.

"If Black Jack escapes the hangman's noose in New Mexico, it will strangle him in Arizona say the officials at the headquarters of the C. & S. Railroad in Denver.

Black Jack was to have been hanged March 27, but his execution was postponed until April 26, and there is a belief that there will be an effort to respite him. A counter movement to place him on the gallows is on foot. So far as known the order of the court will be carried out and he will be hanged at Clayton April 26. On that date the C. & S. Railroad will furnish a large number of guards to prevent a rescue of the desperado by members of his gang of sympathizers. Reports are circulated in New Mexico that a desperate effort will be made to rescue Black Jack while he is being conveyed from Santa Fe to Clayton. To prevent such a rescue it is probable that his departure from Santa Fe will be secret and when he is in jail at Clayton a heavy guard will be kept around him. The C. & S. will furnish part of the guard; the Territory the rest. It is believed by the officers of the law that Black Jack's sympathizers will attempt a rescue, still, precautions will be taken to thwart any such attempt should it be made.'' (*RATON RANGE*, April 18, 1901)

''This afternoon, at three o'clock Tom Ketchum, alias Black Jack, head of the notorious band of train robbers that held up a train at Folsom, Union county, last year and committed many depredations in New Mexico, Arizona and Texas, left the penitentiary for Clayton, Union county to be hanged there on Friday afternoon. Sheriff S. Garcia of Union county (he had succeeded Sheriff Overby and this was to be his first execution. He was accused of bungling the job because of what happened. He wrote a defense of his case and it appeared in various newspapers in New Mexico and Colorado but he convinced no one. Everybody had a finger in the pie when it came to measuring the rope.), his deputy, J. Lewis of Trinidad, Colorado, Detective H. J. Chambers of Chicago who took charge of the prisoner and will see to it that he will not escape alive should any attempt be made on the part of Ketchum's friends to rescue the train robber. Ketchum was not aware that he was to be taken to Clayton today

131

and it came as a surprise to him at noon. He showed no emotion and made no threats but chaffed good naturedly with the sheriff and his deputies. He is in good physical health and has been a good prisoner. He non-chalantly bid good-bye to the prison officials. Sheriff Garcia has made all the preparations for the hanging at Clayton on Friday." (*SANTA FE NEW MEXICAN,* April 23, 1901)

"Tom Ketchum who will occupy a prominent place in the criminal annals of New Mexico as 'Black Jack' train hold-up man and general desperado will expiate his crimes on the gallows at Clayton, Union county, tomorrow (Friday). On Wednesday night's passenger he passed through Raton from Santa Fe where he has been confined in the penitentiary pending the day of his execution, enroute to Clayton. There were fears that friends of the convicted man would attempt his rescue, so there was a strong guard composed of the sheriff of Elbert county, Colorado, and Deputy W. H. Reno, special agent of the C. & S. Railroad, Harry Lewis of Trinidad, Sheriff Garcia of Union county and Tom Grey, his deputy, and Frank Hill and Dan McKee of Raton. A special train of the C. & S. met the prisoner and guard at Trinidad and immediately left for Clayton, arriving there safely." (*RATON RANGE,* April 25, 1901)

The train arrived in Clayton at 5:30 a.m. while the city slept. No one was at the depot. Dawn was about to break. Quietly prisoner and guards walked to the jail. Ketchum noticed the scaffold and asked if he might not inspect it since it was built for him. He looked about the stockade put up for those who had special tickets to the execution. He resented the idea that a limited number of people should see the hanging. He wanted everybody there. Or did the stockade mean less of a chance for escape? He said they ought to test the scaffold first by hanging Harrington; then they could hang him. He was bitter toward Harrington to the end not because the conductor was responsible for the loss of his arm but because of the way he bragged about stopping Black Jack Ketchum. He had the same contempt for Kirchgraber. He repeatedly expressed a wish to see them in hell and was convinced that he would. He slept most of that day and enjoyed a chicken dinner that evening. No one was allowed to visit him. Shortly after supper the sheriff received a telegram to postpone the hanging for another thirty days at the request of President McKinley. The sheriff got in touch with Governor Otero who told him that he never sent the telegram. It was a trick of some prankster or some of Ketchum's friends awaiting an opportunity to free him. Otero called Captain L. C. Fort at Las Vegas and told him to go to Clayton as his personal representative to see that the order of the court be carried out. The telegram did delay the hanging several hours. Eight o'clock was the time appointed for the hanging. It took some time for the matter to be cleared up and for the sheriff to be convinced that the telegram was a phoney. From the jail window Ketchum watched some men putting the finishing touches on the scaffold. He ate a hearty breakfast and waited. Albert W. Thompson, who owned the Clayton newspaper, was permitted to interview him. He spoke of the usual things—hell, Kirchgraber and Harrington. He said nothing about himself or his family. He consented to two pictures. One he asked to be sent to Lee Smith in San Saba, Texas; the other to Eva Prodman of Lodi, California. There has been much speculation regarding the Prodman woman. Was she a childhood sweetheart whose family had moved from Texas to California? Was she merely someone who wrote Black Jack during those months he gained weight in jail? Was she in love with him, refusing to marry him until he reformed? Ketchum did not want his sister to have a picture; nor Berry. A Jesuit priest came in from Trinidad. The Ketchum family belonged to the Baptist faith but the priest hoped to offer some consolation to the doomed man. Ketchum politely refused.

"Padre, get me a fiddler. Perhaps we can have a dance together before I die. Anyway, I'll die as I lived. This delay is not too good. I'll be late for supper in hell." The padre said nothing but prayed for Ketchum walking with him to the scaffold and staying with him to the end. J. R. Guyer, the fiddler, called from outside the window:

"What do you want me to play?"

"Just as the Sun Went Down."

Perhaps Geyer knew the selection; maybe not. The reporter was trying to cover too much ground that day and failed to satisfy our curiosity on that score. As Ketchum had a heavy breakfast he was given no dinner. Nor did he ask for any. The stockade was filling up with guests who had the little yellow tickets needed for admittance. The wind began to whip up dust for there were no paved streets in Clayton in 1901. Many of the spectators held handkerchiefs to their noses so as not to breathe in the sand and gravel that spiraled about the stockade. The grime made their eyes smart but there was no thought of backing away from the mild dust-storm.

1:14 p.m. Sheriff Salome Garcia, tall, full-faced, fat rather than stocky, extremely dark of complexion, as dark as a Moor, faced the prisoner. Whatever his feelings he masked them like an Apache brave. Cut off the bigotes and he would very well resemble an Apache. He took the thick gold watch out of the lower pocket on the left side of his vest, looked at the time and said:

"The time is now."

Without a word Ketchum stood up and followed him to the scaffold. At this moment the sun was hidden behind a cloud of dust. It was a fitting day for a mild dust storm. A moment later the blue sky appeared again and it was another early spring day in New Mexico. The crowd was impatient, bleating, caterwauling cawing in the stockade and beyond. Many who had no tickets of admission filled the saloons. Business houses were closed. No one would expect a cantina to close on such a day. Off to the south

134

one could see the figure of a lone rider galloping across the prairie, skirting the town and making straight for the stockade. He rode a beautiful bay horse. Near the jail he slowed to a trot, came to the fence, tied his horse and hurdled the fence. At the gate he presented a ticket of admission. A sheepherder came in behind him. They were the last two to be admitted. The lone rider walked to a spot where he could command a good view of the jail as well as the scaffold. There he camped looking straight at the jail door, neither recognizing nor caring to recognize anyone in the audience. It would have made no difference. Not a soul in Clayton knew the stranger. He was a tall handsome figure of a man, straight as an arrow, neatly dressed, a man accustomed to the great outdoors. His dark eyes shaded by a white, broad brimmed hat, focused on the door from which Ketchum was to emerge. Detectives took note of his white silk neckerchief, corduroy trousers, high heeled boots, big spurs, sleek cheeks. He wore neither beard nor mustache. This answers the description of one man—The Tall Texan. Earlier this month Carver was killed and his brother George wounded. Could he have been the one who sent the fake telegram?

1:16 Ketchum came from the jail flanked by Detective Chambers and Sheriff Garcia. He was dressed in a black suit, white shirt, black tie, hair nicely groomed except for one recalcitrant curl which the wind bobbed back and forth. The only ones showing signs of strain were the guards and detectives. Ketchum looked like a matinee idol and for many there that afternoon no doubt he was. Within six feet of the hard riding stranger the two looked and communicated a mute message. Whatever their eyes said only Ketchum and the stranger knew. On the scaffold Ketchum was still looking at this stranger when the black bag descended. "Hurry up," Ketchum said to Garcia. After the hanging Special Agent Reno and Sheriff Putman and Chambers sought out the stranger to question him but he was gone and never seen in Clayton again. Putman was the sheriff from Elbert county in Colorado. Just what his connection was with the case has never been explained. Ketchum committed no crimes in that county nor was the sheriff slain in Turkey canyon from that county. Why he would interest himself in the stranger is hard to say except in the hopes of receiving reward money should he turn out to be Ben Fitzpatrick. Shortly after this Ben and his lady friend are in the north with the Hole-in-the-Wall Gang. Near Emory Gap a trail loaded with steel rails crashed into an obstruction of fish plates. Perhaps the stranger had sought to derail the train he thought Ketchum was on. He was a day late. Black Jack was already in Clayton. The secret of his departure from Santa Fe was not given the papers until it was certain he was already in Clayton. A loaded Winchester was found in an infrequently used outhouse. It was never claimed. Ketchum's own rifle was presented to Teddy Roosevelt. How did anyone ever think that Ketchum would be permitted the use of an abandoned outhouse? Commented the editor of the *Clayton Enterprise*:

"Clayton is not the handiest town in the world to take a man away from by force. It is said that there are more guns per man in Clayton than in any other town in the United States. The average is said to be three guns for every male inhabitant of the place. The town all last week was a vertitable arsenal. Weapons were in sight everywhere. Rifles stood behind bars of the saloons, leaned against the key racks in the two hotels, peeped above the ribbon counters in the stores, and were carried in the hands of the men actually on guard duty, while every belt held one or two six-shooters, and the only pockets that held no cartridges had holes in them."

There he stands on the scaffold in the little town of Clayton; the town that sprang from the prairie in a country that had no shadow, devoid of picturesqueness, of mystery, alone in its spot almost an orphan of New Mexico, not yet a child of Texas, the pagentry of its short past

136

buried in the wider scope that bowed to Conquistadores, Comanches, prairie schooners, bull wackers, trail drivers, that made a land mark of Rabbit Ear. Here in a land where everything sprawled on the same monotonous level, the same vast brilliant light of day, it required no pull of the imagination to detect the "end of track" days that buried themselves beneath the frontier appearance of the town. Whether the crowd was pro or con they all enjoyed a good hanging. There wasn't a tear or even a near tear in all that assemblage that would afford him a half ounce of sympathy or comfort. There were no tears for Black Jack Ketchum. This was the greatest publicity Clayton was to know in many a day. Later on its school system would become world renowned, but at this moment the world knew Clayton because of that figure in black, with the black bag over his head.

"That's a fine rope" He remarked when ascending the scaffold. It should be. It cost Union county $20.80. Sheriff Garcia had bought it of the chief of police of Kansas City. It was made of the finest Manila hemp and was fifteen feet long. After the execution the sheriff kept it for a souvenir and later gave it to his daughter. Sheriff Garcia had asked the chief of police in Kansas City about the depth of the drop. He prescribed seven feet. Chambers thought that four and a half feet would be sufficient for a man weighing one hundred and ninety - three pounds as Ketchum did. Captain Fort effected a compromise at five and a half feet; the sheriff was not satisfied and decided to make the drop six feet; Fort and Chambers overruled him and the drop was set at five feet nine inches.

"Are you ready?", asked the sheriff.

"Let her go," came the muffled words from under the hood.

The sheriff raised the hatchet and buried it in the rope that held up the trap door. At the same time Ketchum plunged forward. As he predicted he was never hanged. He was executed. His head fell a few inches to the side, scalp facing the feet. The throng was a ghast. It was as if some unseen being took a jagged blade and served the head from the body. All that remained of Black Jack Ketchum was on the ground beneath the scaffold, in two pieces. Photographer White kept his wits about him and took pictures. They have been reprinted often and will continue to be as long as the story of Black Jack is told.

Those who waited in the streets rushed into the stockade after the execution to pick up the discarded tickets as mementoes. They cut little pieces from the rope that released the trap. They sought to clip locks from the severed head. The hangman's rope Garcia claimed as his possession. It was his first hanging and he wanted something to show for it. The undertaker from Trinidad took the head and sewed it back to the body. He did a wonderful job of it. An hour and ten minutes later the open wagon with the white pine box left the jail. Four men hopped aboard and sat on the box. Out by the fence where the stranger had tied his horse a group of native New Mexican women protected themselves from the howling wind, wrapping their shawls tightly about their heads. Their lips were moving. They were telling their beads. This was all the funeral service Black Jack Ketchum was to have. Over in Texas Mrs. Mary Duncan, was on her knees. Ketchum's sister had prayed long, hard and often these many months. The wagon passed by a saloon. The four men and the driver stopped to quench their thirst. They resumed their seats, lit cigarettes and told each other the tale of the man in the box. At the grave Captain Fort asked the undertaker to open the box. He wanted the last re-assurance that Black Jack found peace out there on the lone prairie. No marker; just a mound of earth somewhere away from the town so as not to haunt the good people of Clayton. A half hour later the wagon returned to town and the four men returned to the saloon. Said the editor of the Clayton paper: "Any public grief or private sorrow for Black Jack Ketchum would be

138

maudlin and an affectation, for he was an outlaw, a savage and vicious outlaw. But the time has not yet gone by when courage in itself and for itself has ceased to be a virtue. Courage was the only service Black Jack had left, and his death demeanor to the end was such as can best be expressed in the unpremeditated words of a New Mexico sheriff—'By God, sir, he did it right!' "

People began to question whether or not it was Ketchum that was hung. William Reno, the man who ran away in the Turkey Canyon fight, was the sage of Clayton that afternoon. "It was the notorious Black Jack beyond a doubt", he said. "I have run to earth the notorious outlaw and his gang. I have worked for years to break up this gang. There was but one Black Jack and he is dead. Most of what Ketchum told in his last interview was a lie. There are a great many things he did not tell. As far as his threats are concerned, they don't amount to much. John Legg wrote me in 1897 that Black Jack was coming north. He was killed in the following year in Fort Sumner. Ketchum says his ghost will haunt Kirchgarber and Harrington. I am not convinced. He says his friends will avenge his death. But his threats don't amount to much. He may have friends at liberty but I noticed they haven't bothered to look him up. Ketchum lied always and he died lying, and I can prove it. He says that it was not his Gang that raided Liberty, New Mexico (present Tucumcari) in 1895. There he lies for he and his brother Sam, have been identified several times from photographic descriptions. When he says that he never committed a crime until 1897, he lies, for he contradicts himself by telling of a murder in which he was implicated the year before. He gets around the case very smoothly by saying that he was told that he resembled Black Jack and might be hanged for that outlaw's crimes." Reno enjoyed every minute of it as he sat at the window of the Pullman car on the way back to Denver. All during the trip he told of his feats of daring against Ketchum and his Gang and was the one who started the ball rolling regarding Ketchum's connection with the Hole in the Wall Gang. Because Ketchum showed knowledge of the train robberies Reno pegged him for the leader of the Hole in the Wall hold-ups. He also places McGinnis and nine others in the Gang. His timing is wrong. Most of these robberies were committed when Ketchum was in western New Mexico, eastern Arizona or jail. Butch Cassidy was not the type to permit Ketchum to run his Gang, nor glorify in his robberies. Reno's rumor which began on the day after the hanging persists to this day. The facts speak for themselves. Beyond one or two possible hold-ups Ketchum was not associated with neither the Hole-in-the-Wall Gang nor the Wild Bunch.

Trinidad News—April 27, 1901: "Berry Ketchum, the brother of the man executed yesterday, declined to take charge of Black Jack's Body, As a result the remains encased in a plain white box were buried in the cemetery at Clayton. All sorts of offers were made by speculators for the outlaw's body. One man particularly insistent in this direction was a Denver, Colorado, man who admitted in a burst of confidence that he was acting for the owners of an eastern museum. The grave for the present will be carefully guarded. The dead outlaw had many admirers. The manner in which he went to his death has appealed to the hero worshipping element and strangers who might be tempted to disturb the remains of the dead outlaw without permission, would meet with serious opposition. Although the men who took part in the apprehension, conviction and execution of Black Jack say that they do not believe that there will be a vengeance, others are not so sanguine."

Santa Fe New Mexican—April 27, 1901: "The Denver Post this afternoon publishes the following dispatch from Sheriff Garcia of Clayton in answer to one asking if the severing of Black Jack's head was caused by the bungling work of the sheriff or in the criminal's throwing himself down to meet the force of a jerk of the rope and thus

140

cause instant death—Said the sheriff: Tom Ketchum's head being severed from his body was caused by his being a very heavy man. Nothing out of the ordinary happened. There were no bungles whatever. Everything worked nicely and in perfect order.''

The decapitation of Ketchum could hardly be recognized as of ordinary occurrence. Of all the men hanged in Arkansas by order of Judge Parker not one had his head severed from his body. When Miller, Allen and two others were hung by the mob in Oklahoma none lost their heads. One would say this was very much out of the ordinary. Butch Cassidy never said one way or the other how he felt about the death of Ketchum. Their association was not as close knit as Ben Kilpatrick, Carver, McManus, Franks and a few others who knew each other as boys in Texas. Not everybody in Clayton wanted Ketchum to hang. Hanging was all right for horse thieves, they reasoned, not for a man who tried to hold-up a train. Such a man belonged in prison. It seemed unjust to them to put a man to death for attempted train robbery when so many horse thieves were running loose. To say nothing of rustlers. There were lots of train robbers in prison, why weren't they hung? While they sympathized with Ketchum they did nothing to save him. As with Billy the Kid, Tom Ketchum stirred controversy and will do so to the day neither of these outlaws will have a following. The Denver Post for November 26, 1950, carried this item: ''The author of the story about Black Jack Ketchum (*EMPIRE MAGAZINE,* October 8, 1950) indicates that he was decapitated by the hanging. I am an old retired printer and worked quite a lot for the Clayton, N. M. *News,* a weekly. While there I saw in the window of a tavern a photo of Ketchum's execution and the photo showed his body hanging. He would not have hanged had he been decapitated. And another thing: All the time I was in Clayton I never heard of a Boot Hill in or near the town. Dodge City has the Boot Hill . . . '' (W. B. Byrd) ''I was a small boy in Trini-

141

dad and heard Frank Harrington tell my father of Black
Jack Ketchum's train hold-up of the C. & S. As I remember the story, Harrington stood close to the partly opened
car door, shotgun in hand, and watched Black Jack and
the engine crew working with the coupling. Harrington
kicked open the door and fired from the hip and Black
Jack fired back just as quick with his .30-.30 Winchester.
The bullet slightly burned Frank's left arm. The story
in Trinidad at the time was that Black Jack was not
caught by a posse but flagged a freight train after the
hold-up. He was suffering so much from his wounds that
he had to give himself up and the authorities took charge
of him at Folsom.'' (G. F. Bateman)

Amarillo Sunday Globe News—July 24, 1955 ''I
(George Hayden) saw them hang Black Jack. No, they
really didn't hang him. He got his way, but he died by the
rope—just as dead as if he had been hanged. Worse than
hanging, to my way of thinking. Back then not many folks
knew that Black Jack had any other name. His real name
was Thomas E. Ketchum. Strange thing, Black Jack was
not sentenced for any of the fifteen murders he was accused of—not for any of that outlawing he and his gang
did in Texas, Arizona and New Mexico, not even for the
cold-blooded shooting of that mother and child. Death
sentence was passed for 'assault upon a railway train,
with intent to commit felony.' Those are the exact words.
Like I said, Black Jack kept declaring no law was power-
ful enough to hang him. That made folks think his gang
was planning rescue. I guess that was why the sheriff
over in Clayton asked every peace officer in the county to
be in Clayton April 26, 1901—Clayton, New Mexico, I
mean. That is where Black Jack was in jail. Anyway,
Salome Garcia, that was the sheriff's name, got word to
Jack Ellison, deputy sheriff of Hartley county, in the
Texas Panhandle, telling him to be sure to get there. Jack
asked me to go along with him; guess he wanted someone
to talk to on that long ride. He did clear up something for

me; explained why Black Jack failed on that last hold-up he staged. It looked like a sure thing, I guess. Black Jack and his Gang had robbed this Fort Worth & Denver express (then it was known as the Colorado & Southern) twice before at this same spot between Twin Mountain and Des Moines. Maybe the train crew were watching, anyway, the train stopped a bit quicker this time; stopped as they rounded the curve. I guess the fireman was really trying to uncouple the train. I know I would have been trying with Black Jack holding a gun on me, but being on a curve made it hard to get the coupling pin out like Black Jack said for him to do. This gave Conductor Harrington his chance. He really had gotten tired of having his train robbed so he shot Black Jack in the arm. We speculated some about why Black Jack didn't get away still, he got back to his horse, but tracks showed the horse never would let him get on. It was pitch dark before we got to Clayton, so we just stabled our horses and found a bed. Next morning any bum dropping off the train in Clayton would have known right straight that something was going to happen. He would have wished he had gone on, the way everybody was eyeing everybody else. Then there was that hammering and sawing over by the courthouse. I hadn't thought much about it until then, but that hit me hard. Men building a scaffold—a scaffold to hang a man. Lots of muttering on the street—'Black Jack never robbed anybody but the filthy rich.' 'Recon Black Jack's Gang is really coming?' ''What you asking me for? I ain't one of them, but Black Jack loaned lots of us poor fellows money; never did hound us to get it back, either.'' Being a deputy, Jack Ellison wasn't missing any of this talk. 'Let's hunt up Salome Garcia and report. Guess I ought to help with the sawing. Hell of a job, though.' I think Ellison was glad to see the scaffold was almost finished. It looked more like a windmill tower, tall, for Black Jack was over six feet. Side timbers and floor were heavy. There was a trap door sawed through the

143

flatform—floor I called it. The trap was fastened up with two rope hinges on one side and only one rope holding it up on the other side. That was the rope they were going to cut to spring the trap. A sharp ax was up there, all ready for use. Talk was different around the court house. 'Black Jack ate all his breakfast. Said it was breakfast in Clayton and supper in hell.' 'Black Jack says he wants his right arm back when he gets to hell; wants it ready to use shoveling coals on Conductor Harrington when he gets down there . . . says he will save some of the coals for the doc who amputated his arm, too.' Everything looked ready but nothing happened. Things got plenty tense when it leaked out the sheriff had a telegram from the governor delaying the execution. Somebody was seeing Black Jack's Gang around every hitching post in town, still—just plain nothing happened. It was over pretty soon after the sheriff found out that telegram was a fake. They led Black Jack up onto the scaffold. His left arm tied behind him; empty right sleeve tucked in his coat pocket. He had on a nice new suit and a bow tie. Black hair all brushed smooth, clean shaved, he looked every inch a fine fellow as he stood there. A deputy helped the sheriff slip the noose in place. Black Jack twisted his neck around, said something and they eased the noose up higher on his neck. Black Jack flung his head up high then, bowed to the sheriff and shouted out loud enough to have been heard across the tracks—'Now let her go.' Guess what happened there! Sure enough they did not hang Black Jack after all. I don't know whether it was what Black Jack planned or not, but just as the sheriff chopped that one rope Black Jack stooped down and threw his two hundred pound weight forward. You know what happened then? That rope cut off Black Jack's head. It rolled to the edge of the platform and then fell down in the dirt. The headless body fell straight through the trap, stood there under the scaffold about a second or two, then twitched and fell, flopped around just like a chicken with is head

144

cut off. You ask me, that's worse than hanging. Folks just stood there a minute, then lots of them turned away real quick. The men waiting with the coffin in a spring wagon helped put Black Jack's body in the coffin after the officers had wiped as much of the bloody dirt off the head as they could get off. They said the head fitted on real nice. They then drove off toward the cemetery south of town. Ellison and I got our horses and started home. Seems like we didn't want anything to eat before we left town. We just rode along quiet most of the time. What can you say after a thing like that?"

The old cemetery was a mile east of Clayton. It was established in February 1889 because the saloon keeper Williams died of delirium tremens and the spot where he was buried was the first likely one the pallbearers found. Red, the partner killed by Charles Meredith, was buried next to Williams. Others came with the years. There were about sixty in this cemetery when it was abandoned in 1907. During the passage of years Black Jack became a legend. Tourists hunted his grave but couldn't find it. Petitions were gathered for the removal of the body to a spot easily accessible to tourists. A committee was appointed to take charge of exhuming the corpse. Mrs. E. Porter, H. H. Errett, C. Eklund, I. Pennington, L. Taylor, T, Gray, R. Isaacs, J. Potter, A. Thompson were to assume the responsibility and conduct the removal of the remains in the best interest of Clayton, Governor Otero in his book, MY NINE YEARS AS GOVERNOR, tells the story of what transpired that day: "The notorious train robber was buried in the old cemetery north of Clayton (*The Trinidad Chronicle News* said it was east of Clayton; the *Enterprise* said it was south—perhaps the Springer Stockman may have west—this is what makes for controversy) In 1933 the owner of the cemetery, by permission, moved the body to the new cemetery. The disinterment was made on the afternoon of Sunday, September 10. It was a beautiful day and fully fifteen hundred curious citizens and strangers from every direction gathered for the occasion. It took two hours of careful work before workmen, under the supervision of undertaker F. P. Kilburn, struck the outside box (as far as it is known there was only one pine board box for Ketchum). Meanwhile, Mr. H. H. Errett, of Clayton, mounted on a truck nearby, told the story of Black Jack's history. When the top of the coffin was removed, the remains of the outlaw were found in a remarkable state of preservation after over thirty-two years. His black hair and long thick mustache had turned a maroon red. His black suit still covered his body, but it turned to a red-gray color. After having been viewed by the public, the remains were transferred to a new grave in the Clayton cemetery, where it, today, attracts thousands of visitors." p. 127)

BIBLIOGRAPHY

Colfax County Docket and Criminal Records

Colfax County Land Claims

Report of the Governor to the Secretary of Interior
1893 to 1901

Walter, P. New Mexico, Land of Sunshine 1906

Otero, Miguel A. My Nine Years as Governor, Albuquerque, 1940

Chase, M. M. The Battle in Turkey Canyon—Unpublished
Manuscript.

Hayden, George, Then Black Jack Was Dead, Amarillo
Globe News, July 24, 1955

Titsworth, B. D., Hole-in-the-Wall Gang, True Magazine
December 1956; February 1957

Bartholomew, Ed, Kill or Be Killed, Houston, Texas 1953

Bartholomew, Ed, Black Jack Ketchum, Last of the Holdup Kings, Houston, Texas, 1956

Prairie Cattle Company—Transcript of Records—Possession of author

S. Dorsey Property Records—Possession of author

Denver Post, November 26, 1950

Amarillo Globe, May 24, 1949

Clayton Enterprise—All Issues to 1902

Raton Range—1888 to 1903

Santa Fe New Mexican—1888 to 1903

Trinidad News (Later Chronicle News) 1890 to 1901

Springer Stockman—1888 to 1897

Folsom Metropolitan September 19, 1891

New Mexico Historical Review, April 1948—pp 129 to 132

Thompson, A. W. Those Were Open Range Days, Denver, 1946

Knight, Oliver, Fort Worth, Norman, Oklahoma, 1953

French, Wm., Some Recollections of a Western Ranchman—New York 1928

Webb, W. P., The Texas Rangers, Mass. 1935

Beebe, L. & Clegg, C., Hear the Train Blow, New York, 1952

Cunningham, E. Triggernometry, Idaho, 1952

The Black Range — 1888 to 1898

Farmington Times 1901